PRENTICE HALL INTERNATIONAL

Language Teaching Methodology Series

Classroom Techniques and Resources
General Editor: Christopher N. Candlin

Grammar in Action *Again*

Other titles in this series include

Grammar in Action *Again*

Awareness activities for language learning

CHRISTINE FRANK
MARIO RINVOLUCRI
in association with Pilgrims Language Courses,
Canterbury

ENGLISH LANGUAGE TEACHING

Prentice Hall

New York London Toronto Sydney Tokyo Singapore

First published 1987
This edition published 1991 by
Prentice Hall International (UK) Ltd
66 Wood Lane End, Hemel Hempstead
Hertfordshire HP2 4RG
A division of
Simon & Schuster International Group

Printed and bound in Great Britain by
Page Bros, Norwich

Library of Congress Cataloging-in-Publication Data

Available from the publisher

British Library Cataloguing in Publication Data

Frank, Christine
   Grammar in action again; Awareness activities for
   language learning. – 2nd ed. – (Language teaching
   methodology series; classroom techniques and
   resources)
   I. Title   II. Rinvolucri, Mario   III. Series   428
   ISBN 0–13–362450–1

2 3 4 5   95 94 93 92 91

Contents

List of the new activities featured in this new edition of *Grammar in Action*

(Arranged alphabetically)

Acknowledgements

We have several individuals to thank for introducing us to exercise areas and to individual exercises. Principal among these are:

Bernard and Marie Dufeu

Joan Hewitt

Steve Burrough

Lydia Langenheim

Carlos Maeztu

Lou Spaventa

Caleb Gattegno

Richard Baudains

Jim Wingate

Eve Ogonowski

Saxon Menné

John Morgan

Jean Cureau

Dierk Andresen

Marcia Karp

Mike Lavery

Sue Leather

Barbara Tregear

Tessa Woodward

Michèle Maldonado

Paul Davis

Silvia Stephan

Gerry Kenny

Dick Tahta

Ten years on

Why a new expanded edition of Grammar in Action?

Many of my colleagues, and those I meet on Teacher Training Seminars, have asked this question. They know and have used the book with many different students and in many different situations and were surprised to hear of our new project. This led me to consider why we were so enthusiastic about adding more of the exercises and activities that had become part of our classroom routine to the existing book. I firmly believe, as I did over ten years ago, that personal and emotional involvement in an exercise is vital to the learning process and will ensure the structure or vocabulary being practised is retained far longer by the learner. If we think back over our teaching careers, is it not the names or faces of the students who have touched us emotionally in either a positive or negative way that we still clearly remember today? Deep personal involvement and experience as aimed at in these activities help our students to see shades of language while at the same time using frames and contexts that would be impossible to achieve with mechanical or transformation-type exercises. In classes I've observed, talking to teachers at seminars and looking at new course books, I've been happy to see over the years a real change from very empty exercises to materials that put more emphasis on the learner and her/his personal world. Teachers, once they have taken this step to put the learner in the centre rather than the material, often find generating new activities to suit the specific needs of a group far easier than previously imagined. We certainly found this the case and hence our new expanded edition.

Are the new activities different from the old ones?

This is probably a question that many teachers will ask. In their aims and the requirements asked of students the activities are certainly not different. I have found, however, from my own experience the range of learners' ages, interests, and social and educational backgrounds where these activities work well to be far greater than I had previously realized. It is therefore not that we have expanded our grammatical categories greatly, as we still feel strongly about focusing our attention on the high frequency grammar areas of the language, but we have in our work considered more activities that could work well in a school situation with teenagers as in classes of older participants in further education of one kind or another.

How can I use these activities?

These activities should not be seen as interesting extras to liven up a class or reward a class at the end of a long, tiring session. The student will certainly get indigestion from such a diet. For us, these activities should be fully integrated into the lesson and part of the teacher's normal lesson plan. Teachers can see them as supplementary practice of structures in a framework where the grammar is determined, but the content has to be provided by the student; as an aid to pacing a lesson; as an opportunity to divert from the course book and as a chance to work without vast numbers of photocopies, overhead projectors, cassette recorders, videos etc., that often litter our classrooms. Finally the activities help to encourage a positive atmosphere in the class where awareness of other students will result in tolerance and trust, which for us is the optimal learning situation.

Christine Frank
Bissendorf
November 1990

Who is this new edition of Grammar in Action for?

The book is ideal for you if you have just finished a training course. In its pages you will find numerous 'life-savers' to help pull you through your first term's teaching. Have fun!

The book is also ideal for teacher trainers – here is a way for your trainees to experience methods of encouraging students to practise grammar *and* for them to get to know one another better within the training group.

Owners of the first edition of this book will find that we have now added 40 new activities to it. You may be tempted to re-purchase the book as it is now one and a half times its previous size. You may also find it worthwhile looking again at those exercises you did not use the first time round. *They* will be the same, but maybe *you* have changed.

The key to this book's success

The fundamental idea behind the text is that students are principally interested in one central topic: themselves and, secondarily, others. The book offers you 140 exercises in which students look at themselves from various angles and then at those around them, either in the group or in their circle of acquaintance outside. There is endless fascination in this, particularly for adolescents. The exercises, providing you use them skilfully, will unlock rivers of language from your students, language they both want to produce and to listen to.

Why pry into people's personal lives?

Some teachers feel uneasy with personalised language work. 'What right', they say, 'do we have to ask students to talk so freely about themselves? In my view it is our duty as teachers to offer students the chance to say meaningful, emotionally charged things about themselves in the target tongue, as this is the only way for them to find a way of *being* in the new language. It is not enough for them to 'know' the language or 'have' its structures. To really speak a language they need to live new thoughts in it and express real feelings through it. Only this way can they make it their own and come to live through it, at least to some extent, in the same way as they live through their mother tongue.

If your aim is to teach a form, then you should use fill-the-gap grammar practice activities. If you want to help your students to develop an alternative linguistic way of being then watch them enjoy themselves in the activities offered by this book.

Mario Rinvolucri
Cambridge
November 1990

Introduction

'Though a student may repeat over and over the forms of the language, in doing so he may not be using the language.' Earl Stevick

This statement seems to express the feeling of dissatisfaction that many critical and conscientious language teachers have been showing for some time. This feeling of poor results for the efforts invested could be explained by the fact that very often the language used in the classroom is not real 'language' but some sort of TEFL dialect.

It is clear that the main concern in any kind of teaching is the student and his success in learning. But how often must they feel deep disappointment at their linguistic competence when they have to face the real world in a foreign environment after hours and hours of hard work in language classes? Have they not listened to, read, said or written the right things?

Up until fairly recently, TEFL relied heavily on a systematic approach in which the foreign language was cut up into structural pieces and fed to the student under certain conditions and according to certain principles ('from easy to difficult', 'listening, speaking, reading, writing'). The result expected from this kind of teaching was the formation of language habits which the student, it was hoped, could use freely in the outside world.

We are by no means proposing that the traditional approach is completely wrong, but it must be pointed out that it has serious defects and is, as far as the required variety of mental processes is concerned, incomplete.

The concern of this book is to increase the number of language learning activities that are prevalent in the classroom today. We owe it to the student that his confidence in the language teacher is repaid.

Basic concepts

The methods and aims that are pursued in any textbook depend decisively on the concept of the subject underlying the textbook. It seems that up to now the main emphasis in TEFL has been placed on method rather than on the content of the subject material. We view the learning of a foreign language as

- the acquisition of 'communicative competence' rather than 'linguistic competence'
- language in action and use rather than language as a system of symbols
- mastering a tool rather than looking at it
- ability and command rather than knowledge.

Language is action with which we start and maintain (and sometimes break off) social relationships. The learner must be enabled to grasp and respond to constantly changing situations and these responses must be functionally effective and socially acceptable. So trying to teach a language (i.e. the competence to use it) without any form of social interaction is a contradiction in itself. Secondly, learning through interaction puts the learner where s/he should be, namely at the centre.

What is an awareness activity?

An awareness activity can be seen as a guided exercise where there is still certain control over the students' responses insofar as they cannot do the task without having understood the structure being practised. However, there is no control over the content of the response, so that the student can express his or her own opinion of the world. This adds up to total involvement of the learner's whole person, with total responsibility for what he or she produces in a rather loose framework of predetermined cues.

Here are two examples:

1 *Them and me*
   Structure : Comparatives : ...er than/more ... than/as ... as
   Steps : A.   Divide the class into subgroups of eight. Ask each student to write one sentence comparing each other person in the sub-group to him/herself. Go round helping and correcting.
   B.   Call out one student's name and get the others to read out their sentences about him or her. Repeat the process, calling out other students' names.

2 *Hiding preferences*
   Structure : Present simple — mainly third person
   Steps : A.   Put this list up on the board:

2 places	2 girls
2 people	2 men
2 meals	2 cars
2 books	2 pictures
2 houses	2 pieces of music

   B.   Choose one pair from the list above.
   Suppose you have chosen two places, the first item on the list; silently think of a place you like very much and one you very much dislike.
   Tell the class you are going to describe two places to them and that they are to decide which one you like and which one you dislike.
   Now describe the two places to the class, doing your best not to

reveal your own preference.
C.   Pair the students and ask them to decide which place you like and which you dislike.
D.   The pairs report to the whole group. You tell them the truth.
E.   Repeat steps B to D with a series of students replacing you.

In the above examples, the students are put in situations where they are both using the target structure and finding out new things about each other.

Why awareness activities?

The various types of mechanical drill have been widely criticised in recent years. This is unjustified insofar as the drilling as a language learning method is concerned, because it is necessary for the learner to become acquainted with the unknown and unaccustomed formal patterns of the foreign language. The criticism is justified, on the other hand, with respect to the claim made by the proponents of the structural-behaviourist approach that pattern practice will make automatic the learner's knowledge of the language.

This book has been designed to close the gap between all too mechanical and all too free language practice. In order to achieve this aim, and in order to make it easier for the teacher to slot the book into his programme, its items have been arranged on a structural basis; it then proceeds to make the language activities personal. This is the feature that most textbooks are lacking, although it is the most vital for language learning. Many writers and teachers would maintain that at the most, pseudo-communication is possible in the classroom. This book, however, is intended to make real communication possible by encouraging the learner to contribute new things of personal relevance. This personalisation is also necessary considering the fact that many or most of the learner's utterances outside the classroom will involve him or her personally.

Furthermore, if we consider the students in our classes to be more interesting than the rather cardboard characters found in the more traditional course books, it follows that a real need exists for activities where the students are invited to speak to each other and express their ideas using structures that have already been presented to them. Practising structures in this very personal series of contexts is much more emotionally real than practising them in the make-believe world of a textbook.

Who are the activities for?

The exercises in this book are primarily for elementary to intermediate level students, although in testing we have found them to be useful for revision purposes in groups of advanced students. Most exercises work equally well with groups of young teenagers or adults in a school, language school or evening school situation.

How to use awareness activities

Real communication can only take place in a relaxed atmosphere of mutual trust and confidence. The teacher can work towards it by forgetting the typical teacher role, which often makes him or her appear intimidating to the students. From a partner-like position as 'counsellor' or 'advisor' he will be more helpful to the students' learning process than from a position of power. Furthermore, the atmosphere created by this attitude will also function as a policy which will make the student more willing to reveal details about himself. The teacher can really stress his partner-like relationship with the students by always participating in the activities, by sitting with the students, if possible in a circle and not in front of them or as an observer outside the group, and by helping rather than judging the language produced.

Many of the exercises require pairing or grouping the students. The traditional approach of putting a good student with a weak student should be varied, as two able, confident students working together will react in an entirely different way from when they are given dominant roles in strong/weak pairs. Similarly, two weaker students will feel an obligation to work harder on an activity than they would if they could rely on a partner to produce what is necessary. One possibility for random pairing of the students is to bring in some pieces of string about 30cm. long. The teacher should have one piece of string for every two students. The strings are held by the teacher high above his/her head and the students are told to each take the end of one piece. The teacher lets go, and each student is paired with the person at the other end of their string.

With exercises that have a written stage, it is easy for the teacher to go round the class while the students are writing and help by showing the student where the mistake is but not what it is. The teacher should do this by either sitting or kneeling with the students and not by standing over them in a powerful position. As peer correction seems preferable both for psychological and social reasons, students should be encouraged to seek help and advice from others in the group and only from the teacher when absolutely necessary. Soon, the whole attitude to making mistakes and their correction changes, and all students will profit from co-operation to produce accurate language.

Correction of the oral stage is rather more difficult, as the student should not be interrupted, particularly when emotionally involved. The teacher may choose to note the errors on cards which s/he hands to the individual students at the end of the session, or s/he may use silent finger correction, where s/he can correct word order, indicate wrong tense or where a short form is required, with gestures and in complete silence. Supposing a student speaking to the group says, 'Gerlinde goes sometimes to church.' *Don't* at this point verbally interrupt and provide the correction. Instead, silently stop the student, tap your thumb and say, 'Gerlinde'. Then tap your index finger and silently elicit 'goes' from the student. Now tap your middle finger and elicit 'sometimes'. With the fingers of your other hand, reverse the position of your index and middle fingers, thus showing that the order is wrong. Then get the student to say the sentence correctly. *All this can and should be done in complete silence.* This leaves the student who made the mistake time to think things out and invest enough of himself to make the correction meaningful. (Silent finger correction derives from Caleb Gattegno's *Silent Way*.)

When reading through these activities, a teacher may be deterred from wanting to try them if s/he teaches in small classrooms with heavy furniture. However, by using the aisles and the front of the classroom for milling activities and getting alternate rows of students to turn to face those behind, groups can be formed and real communication can take place in what initially seemed unfavourable conditions.

A further problem for the teacher is what to do if the student says, 'But I can't draw', or, 'I don't want to talk about that.' In cases like these it is absolutely necessary to respect the learner's wishes; this is one of the basic premises of the approach of this book. If individuals do not want to participate actively in a particular language activity it does not necessarily mean a loss for them if they follow by listening to the others.

Although there are many activities in this book which can be used from the outset with a new group of students (see, for instance, the section which follows on Ice-breakers), some require reasonable understanding and trust between teacher and students. We have indicated in footnotes some instances where we feel this to be particularly important and suggest that you do not use these activities until students know each other fairly well. However, it is our firm conviction that by judicious use of activities of the kind described in this book you will reach the stage of mutual trust and confidence much sooner. And your students will be truly *using* the language and not merely repeating its forms.

I
Ice-breakers

Introduction

Ice-breakers are designed to be used when students first come together into a group or when a large new intake joins a group. Ice-breakers are very useful at the start of a secondary school first year language class, when sub-groups of children know each other well from having been to the same primary school. Ice-breakers help to get the children meeting people from beyond their primary clique. They are equally useful when an adult education evening class meets diffidently for the first time. The aim of such exercises is to get people to learn each other's names and become aware of each other as people. Well-chosen ice-breakers help to relax people, get them to unfold their arms, to smile and to laugh.

Name learning does not happen automatically among students — we have been into small classes of fifteen people who had been together for twenty or more hours where the students did not know each other's names. There are even RSA teacher training groups that work together for six months, meeting twice a week, without finding out each other's names.

Ice-breakers, though, do a lot more than teach names. They get the students looking at each other (they may well come with the expectation that they will only have to look at the teacher), wondering about each other, helping each other and laughing together. In doing these exercises people learn a little about other group members consciously and a vast amount unconsciously.

Some teachers may at first feel that doing ice-breakers is just 'playing', somehow a waste of time. In fact, opening with these people-centred exercises is a very powerful communication to the students of an educational philosophy, powerful because it is direct and corporeal, not transmitted through words and intellectualisations. If your course is going to be student-centred, it is vital to get this across from the very first five minutes of the first hour.

You have a double task when conducting and taking part in such opening exercises. On the one hand you must join in the exercises and show yourself as a group member and a human being, and on the other you need to observe the students' reactions and language behaviour. Ice-breakers at post-beginner level upwards give you a pretty good idea where the students are linguistically. If you watch body reactions in the group you will also begin to form an idea of who is pushy, who is shy, who is a potential outsider and so on. Ice-breakers allow you to discover all this at the first class meeting rather than ten weeks into the term.

Ice-breakers are an absolutely necessary preliminary to the exercises in the subsequent sections of this book, many of which cannot be usefully, or in some cases safely, done in an un-warmed-up group. If they don't feel like they are for you, then this book isn't either.

If you want to use more ice-breakers than we suggest here, excellent source books are:

Moskowitz, G. (1978), *Caring and Sharing in the Foreign Language Classroom*, Newbury House

Pfeiffer, J.W. & Jones, J.E. (eds.), *A Handbook of Structured Experiences for Human Relations Training*, Vols. I-VII, University Associates, La Jolla, California

Ignorant introductions

Level   Post-beginner and above

Time   20-40 min.

In class

1   Group the students in clusters of 6 to 8.

2   A student introduces another member of the group to the group, inventing biographical information. The person described can then say how she/he feels about the information and correct it.

Impersonating the other

Level   Post-beginner and above

Time   20-40 min.

In class

1   Group the students in clusters of 6 to 8.

2   Give them ten minutes to find out as much as they can about each other in pairs. Each person works with one partner only.

3   Ask person A from one pair to stand behind person B and introduce B to the group with their hands on B's shoulders. A speaks on B's behalf and uses the first person. B then introduces A to the group in the same way. And so on round.

Acknowledgement

We learnt this introductory technique from Bernard Dufeu.

Timing the truth

Level   Post-beginner and above

Time   10-15 min.

In class

1   Organise the students in threes. Ask them to choose one in each three to start the exercise. Tell the speaker in each group to speak for one minute, introducing him or herself. Nothing said must be true – it must all be lies. You time the minute.

2   Tell each threesome to choose a second speaker. This person is to speak for a minute introducing him or herself. Everything said must be true. Time the minute.

3   Tell the last speaker in the threes to introduce him or herself mixing truth and falsehood. At the end of this minute the students will need time to sort out what was true and what was not.

Variation

The exercise above can be used for many other speaking situations beyond introductions. So for example, you could give the group this topic: *Does God exist?**

- The first speaker gives his/her real opinion about the topic, speaking for two timed minutes.
- The second speaker chooses to speak as a person she knows well, and gives this person's true opinion (two minutes).
- The third speaker mixes her real opinions with false ones (two minutes).

* God is banned from most EFL discourse – this might well be a good reason for bringing him/her in. Perhaps it depends on the composition of your group.

Ball game

Level   Complete beginners and above

Time   5-15 min.

Preparation

Bring 1 to 3 soft balls to class, depending on how many students you have. At a push you can make soft balls with crunched-up newspaper and Sellotape.

In class

1   Have the students stand or sit in a circle. This may mean moving furniture, or if the furniture is fixed to the floor, it may mean people perching on desks and standing between them.

   If there are more than 20 people in the class, make 2 circles. Join one circle yourself and throw a ball to someone opposite you, saying your name as you throw. Gesture to the person who has caught the ball to do the same to someone else, and so on. Get this going in the other circle or circles, simultaneously.

   Let this phase go on longer than the students feel it is necessary so that they really do have time to memorise a good number of the names.

2   Join one of the circles, take the ball and throw it to someone opposite you, but this time say *their* name, not your own. Gesture to the person who has caught the ball to do the same to someone else. Get the same name-retention exercise going in the other circle(s).

Variation

Do the same exercise as above, but throwing an imaginary ball. This forces much more concentration and eye contact.

Acknowledgement

We learnt the ball-throwing introduction technique from a Pilgrims colleague, Jim Wingate, and the variation was shown to us at a British Council seminar in Paris.

Eyes first

Level   Complete beginners and above

Time   5-15 min.

In class

1   To do this exercise you must be able to have people stand in a circle with no furniture in the way. This is an exercise for a group of 10 students or more.

Get everybody's attention fixed on you. Then *stare* at someone opposite you in the circle, beckoning them forward. Walk slowly across the circle towards them, and as you pass, point to yourself and say your name, getting the other person to do the same. Walk on and take the person's place in the circle - they take yours. Motion to another student to repeat the procedure, which continues, no longer led by you.

Make sure that the pair crossing the circle make firm eye contact first. Make sure they say their names loudly enough for other people to hear. Don't have everybody crossing the circle at once, as no one learns anything in the ensuing chaos.

2   Get everybody's attention fixed on you. Stare at someone opposite you in the circle, beckoning them forward. As you reach them in the middle of the circle, offer your hand and say 'Hallo/Hi (+ their name).' They say 'Hallo/Hi (+ your name).' Take their place in the circle, while they take yours. Get the other students doing the same, testing how many names they have learnt.

Acknowledgement
We learnt this technique from Bernard Dufeu of Mainz University.

The answers

Level   Elementary and above

Time   20 min.

Preparation

Have a pin or an adhesive label to give to each student so that they can attach a piece of paper to their clothing.

In class

1   Ask each student to take a sheet of paper and write their name clearly in capitals at the top. Ask the students to sit back and think of all the questions their classmates might want to ask them to start getting to know them. Now ask them to write down *answers* to 10 of the questions they would like to have answered. Tell them to write in large letters and clearly. Short answers are fine.
     A student sheet might look like this:
     Annie Guinard
     ●   French
     ●   in the South of France
     ●   16
     ●   51
     ●   I haven't learnt yet, etc ...

2   Give the students pins or adhesive labels and ask them to pin or stick the sheets with the answers on to their fronts. Ask them to get up and move around the room *in silence*, reading other people's answers. They must *not* talk.

3   After 3 or 4 minutes of answer reading, tell the students they may now speak and question anybody whose answers they did not understand or found intriguing. This often leads to people asking more questions and going beyond the information given in their partner's answers.

Variation

Instead of asking students to write answers to getting-to-know questions you can ask them to draw something that is important to them, leaving it to them what they choose.
If you are working with technicians, ask them to draw the most important piece of machinery in their area of expertise.
If you are working with teachers, ask them to draw the ground plan of a classroom.

Acknowledgement

This exercise is described in Pfeiffer & Jones (eds).

Mime introductions

Level   Post beginner and above

Time   15–30 min.

In class

1   Form the class into groups of about 8 students. Ask the students to find a partner within their group. Now tell the students they have 3–4 minutes to find out as much as they can about their partner but they must *not speak or write* any known language. (This will force them to draw or mime, but don't tell them this — let them work it out for themselves.) If there is an odd number of students you should pair off with the odd one out and mime with him or her.

2   After four minutes, stop the silent pairwork and ask the groups of 8 to re-form. Each student is then to report to the group of 8 what they think they found out about the partner. After each report, allow the person reported on to put right any misinterpretations. This can be very funny — it's the misunderstandings that make for interaction and release laughter. The reports in the different groups of 8 happen simultaneously.

Variation 1

We have presented this exercise as an ice-breaker but it can well be used some way into a course to work on the second and third person of the present simple, as most of the reporting takes this form:

You are married	She likes gardening
Petra doesn't play tennis	She watches a lot of television, etc.

(The reporter sometimes feels like speaking to the group *about* the person, and sometimes feels the need to report back to the person, especially if the mime was unclear.)

Variation 2

Pair the students. A asks B questions verbally but B must only answer in mime,

or

Pair the students. A asks B questions in mime and B responds verbally.

Acknowledgement

Steve Burrough of the Dieppe Chambre de Commerce introduced this exercise to us.

What we have in common

Level   Elementary and above

Time   20 min.

In class

1   Split the class up into groups of about 8. Within these groups, ask people to pair off and find 5 things they have in common with their partner and 5 things they don't have in common. Tell them to note these down.

2   Once the questioning in pairs is over, ask the students to report to their group of 8. The reports in the groups go on simultaneously. If the students are elementary level give them structures to help the reporting, e.g.:

We both like ....
S/he lives in .... but I ....
We are both wearing ....
I prefer .... s/he prefers ....

NB   *In using this exercise as an ice-breaker, don't prescribe structures for the paired questioning. Listening to how they go about this unguided will prove a golden diagnostic opportunity for you.*

Funny greetings

Level   Complete beginners and above

Time   10 min.

In class

You need some space for this exercise, though it *can* be done in a traditional classroom with fixed benches. If you have fixed benches, have the students use the aisles and the back and front of the room.

1   Ask everybody to stand up and move around very slowly. They must avoid eye contact and look at the floor. As they pass another person they say their name to the person quietly, without looking at them.

2   Ask them to look up. They are to move around and shake hands with people, saying their own name.

3   Ask them to go on shaking hands and saying their name, but this time using only the *left* hand.

4   Tell them they all belong to a civilisation that greets by rubbing elbows. They are to rub elbows and say 'Hallo (+ the other person's name).'

5   Tell them they belong to a civilisation that greets by shaking the other person's ear-lobe between thumb and forefinger. Ask them to do this and say 'Hallo (+ the other person's name).'

With beginners or low level students you give the instructions in their mother tongue, or alternatively you mime what you want them to do and they follow you.

Acknowledgement

This is one of the name-learning exercises used by Eve Ogonowski with All's Well students.

Empty chair

Level   Complete beginners and above

Time   5-10 min.

In class

This exercise cannot be done until a name-learning activity has already taken place in the group. Have the students sit in a circle, or in 2 circles if there are more than 20 of them. Introduce an empty chair into each circle. Ask the student who has the empty chair on their right to name another student and ask them to come and sit in the chair, e.g.:

'Petra, come and sit next to me.'

This automatically leaves an empty chair elsewhere in the circle. The person who has the vacant chair on their right names another student and invites them over, etc ...
If there is only one circle, you can be in it — if any group member is being left out, quietly invite them to sit next to you when your turn comes round.

Acknowledgement

We first heard of this technique from Bernard Dufeu of Mainz University.

True names and false professions

Level   Elementary and above

Time   10-15 min.

In class

Organise your students into seated circles of 10-14 people. Join one of the circles and give your real name and a false profession, an imaginary profession. Designate another person in the circle. This person must first introduce you and your imaginary profession to the group, and *then* him/herself to the group with a false professsion. This student then designates another who repeats the process, first introducing you and then the first student and then him/herself, etc...

Get this process going in all the circles in the room.

The last person to introduce him/herself has quite a lot of names and imaginary professions to remember!

Variations

If your class is advanced you may want to pick some set that is more restricted than professions. You could ask everybody to give their own name and a *fish*, or their own name and a *tree*.

This exercise type is mentioned in *Learning English Words*, by John Morgan, Mary Glasgow Publications, 1984. The suggestion here is that people should name containers, e.g.: 'I'm John and I'm a flowerpot.'

This frame can also be used to get people practising a structure. You might ask the students to give their names and to say one thing they have never done, e.g.: 'I'm Mario and I've never killed anybody.'

If you are working with a group of colleagues on a training course you can ask them to give their names and false reasons for having come on the course; e.g.: 'I'm Yukiko and I like wasting my time.'

Acknowledgement
Lou Spaventa taught us this warm-up technique.

Forced choices

Level Elementary and above

Time 20 min.

In class

1 You need an open space for this exercise and it does not work well with a group of less than 20.

Have people push the furniture back against the walls and all stand in a tightly packed group in the centre of the floor.

Tell them they are going to have to make a choice between 2 alternatives and if they choose one they will go to one end of the room and if the other, to the other end of the room. When they get to their end of the room ask them to pick *one partner* and explain their choice to this person. When they have finished explaining they should pick another partner and explain again. Emphasise that they should always be working in pairs, not small groups. (This makes the work much more intensive.)

2 Now give them the first forced choice:

'Everybody who feels like a waterfall, go to the blackboard end of the room.'

'Everybody who feels like a lake, go to the other end of the room.'

3 Don't let the pair work drag on too long. After about 2 or 3 minutes ask the 'waterfalls' to advance across the room and take a 'a lake' partner and again explain their choices.

4 Bring the students back into a tight group in the centre of the room and give them a new forced choice, e.g.:

CAT	DOG
BREAKFAST	DINNER
INTROVERT	EXTROVERT
RED	YELLOW

Variation

Ask a student to come out and run the group, proposing forced choices which s/he can think up.

Acknowledgement

Carlos Maeztu, now a teacher trainer for Northrop in Saudi Arabia, taught us this exercise. It comes from the values clarification area, and an exellent introduction to this thinking is Smith (1977).

Home town

Level   Elementary and above

Time   15-20 min.

Preparation

Bring one very large sheet of paper to class for each group of 6 students, plus a felt-tipped marker per group of 6. Bring Blu-tack or drawing pins to hang the papers on the walls.

In class

1   Divide the class into sixes and give each sub-group a large sheet of paper to hang on a wall in their part of the room, and a felt-tipped marker.

2   Ask the groups of 6 to find out in which part of the country or in which countries each group member was brought up.
Ask each group to draw a map or maps to include these areas.

3   Now, with the groups working simultaneously, ask one student per group to place their home town or village on the appropriate map and to write in their name over the name of the homeplace.
This student then tells the other 5 members of their group something about the homeplace and their feelings for it. This speech should not last more than one minute.

4   Step 3 is repeated by every other member of each sub-group.

NB   *If everybody in a sub-group turns out to have been brought up in the same city, then the map will show the districts of that city.*

Acknowledgement

The home town idea is an ice-breaker suggested in Pfeiffer & Jones (eds.).

Strong or gentle?

Level   Elementary and above

Time   20-30 min.

In class

1   You can only use this exercise if nobody in the class yet knows anybody's name and if the students are old enough to have a firm idea of how a graph works.

Organise the students in groups of 12-15. Ask each student to write their name on a bit of paper and to give the paper to one person you designate in each group. The paper-gatherers then write up the names of the people in their group on the board and number them.

2   Ask each student to draw a graph with a GENTLE axis and a STRONG axis. Ask each student to plot the names in their group on their graph according to whether they find the names more strong or gentle. The numbers next to the names on the board will help with the graphing, e.g.:

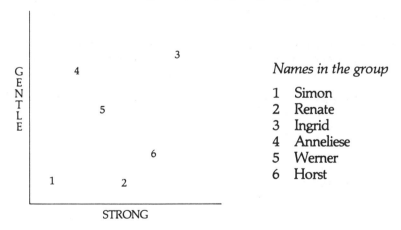

Names in the group

1   Simon
2   Renate
3   Ingrid
4   Anneliese
5   Werner
6   Horst

3   When the students have completed their graphing, get them up and moving about the room. Ask them to pair off and explain their graphing of the names to other people in their own group. Naturally in this process they will also find out which name belongs to whom.

Acknowledgement

This is an adaptation of an exercise for learning vocabulary from a reading passage in Morgan and Rinvolucri (1984).

All the words you know

Level   Absolute beginners

Time   20-30 min.

In class

1　Explain in the students' mother tongue that you suspect they already know quite a lot of English words. Ask them to work alone and write down all the English words they do know. Encourage the ones who look blank. Don't let the students help each other.

2　Ask them to work in pairs, checking out each other's lists and adding to them.

3　Invite them to work in fours, enriching their lists.

4　Get them to compare lists in groups of 8.

5　Have a 'secretary' come to the board and write down the words the people in the groups dictate to them. The secretary will fill the board with the English words the group actually do know, to the students' amazement. Make sure that students proposing words explain their meaning to the others in the mother tongue.

NB   *Since exposure to English in informal situations is quite frequent in many countries you can only do this exercise with complete beginners. Even slightly false beginners will know so many words that they will overflow the frame of the exercise.*

If you don't believe your complete beginners will know some words of English, try the exercise on page 24.

Rationale

This is one of a group of ice-breaking exercises in which people get to know each other by rubbing elbows and focussing side by side on a common task, rather than by staring into each other's eyes and asking premature questions. We might well use this type of initial exercise if teaching in a place like Finland, where people tend to come into a group shyly.

Variation

If you have false beginners or higher level students you can still do this kind of exercise, but you must limit the set of words they have to find:
'All the words you know to do with the house.' the car.' childbirth.'

Acknowledgement

We learnt this exercise from John Morgan, a Pilgrims colleague.

Japanese word search for you, the teacher

We are assuming that you are a complete beginner in Japanese.

Write down all the words in Japanese you already know in the space below; trade names like Toyota are not allowed:

1	11
2	12
3	13
4	14
5	15
6	16
7	17
8	18
9	19
10	20

When you find you can get no further, turn the book upside-down.

How many martial arts words did you find?

Did you think of a special word for a woman?

Something a woman wears?

Words to do with theatre, poetry, religion?

Did you find a term for a warrior and an Emperor?

Food? Wine? Way of dying?

The names for Japanese scripts?

The word for Japan?

Flowers?

Paper-folding?

Dwarf trees?

By numbers

Level   Complete beginners and above

Time   5-10 min.

In class

You need to be able to push the furniture to the walls for this exercise. It's not feasible with a group smaller than 20. Have everybody milling in the centre of the room. Tell the students to get into groups of 5 and to introduce themselves in low voices.

- Tell them to make groups of 7 and shout their introductions;
- groups of 4 and whisper their introductions;
- groups of 8 and introduce themselves in a friendly way;
- groups of 3 and introduce themselves in a sleepy way.
- Tell the whole group to introduce themselves very slowly.

If you are working with beginners or low level students, the instructions are given in L1.

Acknowledgement

We learnt this technique from Saxon Menné.

Choosing a country

Level   Elementary and above

Time   10-15 min.

Preparation

Draw outlines of 7 countries on large sheets of paper or card and cut these out. Choose countries that have an image for your students or countries to which some of them may have been. Take Blu-tack to class so you can stick the country outlines up round the walls.

In class

1   Stick the country outlines up round the walls. Go round making sure that all the students can see them and can identify them.

2   Ask the students to go and stand by the country they like best, take a partner and explain their choice. If there are only one or two people standing by a given country, get them to team up with another minority group.

3   When the exchange of information is beginning to die down, remove the 2 countries that have the most people round them. Say that these 2 are out of the game and ask the people round them to make a second choice and go to another country. They are to explain their second choice to the people who are there because of their first choice.

Acknowledgement
We learnt this technique at a seminar in the Living Languages Dept. at the University of Leuven.

II

Student Questionnaires and Interviews

Introduction

We have devoted a whole section of this book to techniques for getting students to ask questions as we feel this skill to be vital to them in getting a grip of the foreign language. In most classrooms students spend a lot of time answering the teacher's questions but not nearly enough asking each other questions and finding out more about each other.

Some of the exercises in this section lead into the students freely writing their own questionnaires. You can add to the interest and excitement of this by letting the students know that you want to use their questionnaires with another, lower class. This will make the correction work on the questionnaires feel worthwhile. The idea of one set of students creating materials for another group is a very useful one.

Students get bored with always working with the people in their own class, and a very good way of alleviating this feeling of staleness is by pairing off people from Class A with those from Class B and getting them to do an exercise like the questionnaire on grandparents.

You will find plenty of exercises beyond those we give here for getting students to ask each other questions in other books. For example, Moskowitz (1978) has an excellent exercise called *Search for Someone who* ... Each student is given a sheet that looks like this:

Search for Someone who ...
  1   likes to garden
  2   owns a bicycle
  3   plays the piano etc.

There are 25 items like this on the sheet. The students get up and rush round trying to find people who ... Whenever they find a person with the given attribute they jot down his/her name next to the item. The 'winner' is the person to collect most names.

Once you have got into the swing of these exercises you will probably find that plenty more come to mind, ones that no one before you has thought of.

Two minute inquisitions

Level   Elementary and above

Time   20 min.

Grammar structures   A mixed bag of interrogatives

In class

1   Divide the class into sub-groups of 8 to 10 people. Have an extra chair in each group.

2   Ask one person to sit in the empty chair and to answer all the questions her group manage to ask her in 2 minutes. Another group member times the period. If there are questions the hot seat person does not want to answer, she just says *pass*. Each student spends two minutes being questioned by the others.

NB   *You can use this exercise as an ice-breaker with an extrovert sort of group. You can also use it some way through a course, when people have lots of things they wonder about others but do not always put into words.*

Acknowledgement
We learnt this at a Cambridge Academy staff meeting.

Roles I'm in

Level Elementary and above

Time 30-45 min.

Grammar structures Mixed interrogatives

In class

1 Give the group this list of roles:

friend	bully
daughter	manager
brother	victim
enemy	class-mate
helper	colleague
parent	voice of conscience
son	playmate
cousin	husband
wife	lover
agent	conciliator
middle man	joker

Explain unknown words. Ask the students to add any other roles they can think of.

2 Ask each student to choose six roles they can adopt. They write three questions, *addressed to themselves*, about each of the six roles. So a student called Mary might write: 'Mary, are you a good X?'

3 Ask the students each to choose a partner. They exchange questionnaires and the partner puts the questions the writer wrote for herself to her. She answers. The same then happens the other way round.

One question – many answers

Level   Post-beginner and above – the exercise is particularly useful with mixed ability classes

Time   15-20 min.

Grammar structures   Present simple interrogative and declarative, future perfect interrogative + declarative (contracted forms) + by, prepositions

In class

1   Ask a student to sit with you in front of the class. He or she repeats the same question while you give as many varied answers as possible. With *where do you live?* as the insistence question the dialogue might go like this:

>   *Student:*   Where do you live?
>   *Mario:*   In the far west of Europe.
>   *Student:*   Where do you live?
>   *Mario:*   In south east England.
>   *Student:*   Where do you live?
>   *Mario:*   Well . . . in a medium-sized town, about 4½ kms from the city centre . . . etc.

The teacher continues the dialogue for another dozen answers.

2   Pair the students and ask them to question and answer as you have done. If the group is very heterogeneous, have the weaker students ask the repeated questions.

Here are some more questions that have worked well for us:

- *Who are you?*
- *How do you study?* ('Study' could be replaced by any other verb designating a centrally important activity).
- *What frightens you?*
- *What is inflation?* (Excellent with ESP groups of economists.)
- What'll you've done by the year two thousand and five? (With this one you need to supply the students with some of these answer forms):

- I'll probably've . . .
- I may well've . . .
- I'm not sure whether I'll've . . .

You should insist on full, natural contractions.

Variation

Ask two students, A and B, to work in front of the whole group. A asks B the same question repeatedly:

● *Why do you like X-ing?*

B gives a different answer each time. They both know what X stands for but the group does not. They listen to the answers and try to guess.

Rationale

Insistence questioning is a creativity technique that allows the person answering to really stretch their language and their thinking. Oddly, it is also a creative exercise for the questioner whose role is very important to the person answering. If the questions sound aggressive or inappropriate it is hard for the other to go on.

What normally happens is that the questioner starts experimenting with volume, intonation, tone and look, so as to stay in rapport with their partner.

Acknowledgement

We learnt this technique from Marjorie and Richard Baudains, authors of Alternatives, *1990.*

Gifts

Level   Intermediate

Time   20 min.

Grammar structures   Interrogatives, all tenses

Preparation

Prepare the following questionnaire:

(A)
1   When do you give somebody a present?
2   Are there any traditional presents you give in your country, e.g. for a wedding or when somebody moves into a new home?
3   Do you like to give or receive home-made presents?
4   ....
5   ....

(B)
1   When do you normally receive presents?
2   Do you ever give things to eat or drink as presents?
3   What is the nicest thing you have ever been given?
4   ....
5   ....

In class

1   Get the students to define the word 'present'.
    (You may also bring in an English–English dictionary or prepare an overhead projection foil of this entry, so that the students can compare their own definition with the 'official' one.)

2   Pair the students and give one questionnaire A and the other questionnaire B.

3   Ask the students to read the questions and write two additional ones.

4   Student A asks question 1, student B answers it and asks her/his question 1 to student A. They continue until all the questions have been asked/answered.

5   Each student reports back some item from the interview.

Simple pair-work questionnaire

Level   Elementary and above

Time   50 min.

Grammar structures   Contrasted 'do' and 'did' questions

Preparation

Copy the questionnaire below enough times to give one to each pair in your class.

In class

1   Teach them the terms *paternal* and *maternal* grandparents and any words from the questionnaire they won't know.

2   Pair the students and give out the Grandparents questionnaire. Student A puts all the questions to B and then Student B puts all the questions to student A.

3   Ask the students, still in pairs, to make up their own Grandparent questionnaire. Tell them to make 2 copies (one each) of their new questionnaire.

4   Pair the students differently so they can try out their new questionnaires on each other.

Grandparents questionnaire

- How many grandparents have you got alive today?
- How old are they/how old were they when they died?
- How many children do they/did they have?
- How old were they when they got married?
- Do they/did they live alone?
- What do/did your grandparents do all day?
- Where do/did your grandparents go on holiday?
- How often do you/did you see your grandparents?
- Which of your grandparents do you/did you feel closest to?
- How do you imagine yourself as a grandparent?

Danger

Avoid treating this subject area if you know that someone in the group has recently lost a grandparent.

Acknowledgement

The idea for a grandparent questionnaire was prompted by Wattenmaker & Wilson (1980).

Role-reversed pair-work questionnaire

Level   Intermediate and above

Time   30 min.

Grammar structures   The 'second' conditional

Preparation

Copy the questionnaire on pages 30 and 31 so you can give one copy to each of your students.

In class

1   Pre-teach *some* of the words they won't know in the questionnaire.

2   Pair the students. Give out the questionnaires and tell the students to work *on their own*, silently, answering the questionnaires *as their partner*. If John and Mary are paired, John answers the questionnaire *as Mary* and she answers it *as him* — they do not talk to each other while doing this. You go round helping with difficult words.

3   The partners work together and explain the choices.

'How you show your feelings' questionnaire

If you don't think your partner would choose any of the alternatives in a given question, then write in what they *would* do on the dotted line.

1   If you had waited too long in a queue to buy a rail ticket, would you
    - complain bitterly to the other people in the queue
    - hold your feelings in and say nothing
    - leave the queue
    - .....?

2   If an accident was about to happen, would you
    - mumble
    - yell
    - say nothing
    - .....?

3   If a letter arrived saying you had passed an important exam, what would be your first reaction?
    - jump about the house and shout at the top of your voice
    - ring a friend
    - grin quietly to yourself
    - .....?

4   If you were afraid, would you
    - whisper
    - scream
    - shout
    - .....?

5   If your boss wanted you to work overtime, would you
    - accept with alacrity
    - roundly refuse
    - accept but grumble behind his/her back
    - .....?

6   If you were told that someone you loved had died, would your first reaction be to

- stay silent
- sob
- weep quietly
- shriek your grief
- .....?

7   If someone accused you of dishonesty, would you

- bawl them out
- question them acidly
- shrivel up and say nothing
- .....?

8   In church, would you

- drift off into your own thoughts
- observe others
- pray
- .....?

9   If you saw a friend looking down in the dumps, would you

- try to ignore it
- attempt to cheer them up
- ask them what the matter was
- .....?

10 If you suddenly realised you had left your passport at home just as you were arriving at the airport on your way to a holiday abroad, would you

- kick yourself mentally for being a fool
- mumble with rage
- stay completely calm
- curse out loud
- panic
- .....?

Multi-person questionnaire

Level   Elementary and above

Time   20 min.

Grammar structures   The 'second' conditional

Preparation

Copy the questionnaire opposite so you can give one copy to each person in your class.

In class

1   Pre-teach any new words in the questionnaire.

2   Give out the questionnaire and tell the students the questionnaire is about them and 2 other members of their family. Tell them to choose which 2 members they wish to work round and to fill in these relations in the gaps in the questionnaire.

3   Pair the students. They put the questions to each other.

Homework

Ask them to write a new questionnaire designed to provoke as *different* as possible reactions in them and their two family members.

In the next class

1   Pair the students and ask them to exchange questionnaires.
2   Student A puts student B's questions to him/her, and vice versa.

Questionnaire

A If you saw something on fire in the house, what would you do?
B If your _____ saw something on fire in the house, what would they do?
C If your _____ saw something on fire in the house, what would they do?

A If your boss asked you to work at the weekend, what would you do?
B If their boss asked them to work at the weekend, what would
   your _____ do?
C If their boss asked them to work at the weekend, what would
   your _____ do?

A If you were walking at night and suddenly heard a cry, what would you do?
B What would your _____ do in a similar situation?
C What would your _____ do in a similar situation?

A If you lost your job, what would you do?
B If your _____ lost his/her job, what would s/he do?
C If your _____ lost his/her job, what would s/he do?

A If you were alone and feeling bad, what would you do?
B In the same situation, what would your _____ do?
C In the same situation, what would your _____ do?

A Suppose someone offered you drugs, what would you do?
B What would your _____ do?
C What would your _____ do?

A If you could be more successful abroad than in your own country would you
   emigrate?
B Would your _____ emigrate in this situation?
C Would your _____ emigrate in this situation?

A If an unknown person invited you to their house, what would you do?
B What would your _____ do?
C What would your _____ do?

A future/past questionnaire

Level   Elementary and above

Time   30 min.

Grammar structures   Past simple/present perfect

In class

1   Ask each student to think silently about him/herself in 20 years' time. What will he/she have done, seen, achieved/not achieved etc. by then? Allow the students at least 5 minutes to collect their thoughts.

2   Tell the students they are going to move forward in time 20 years and write the date on the blackboard, e.g.:

It's May 20th, 2012.

3   Pair the students and ask each to interview the other about the 'last 20 years' of his/her life.

Students are likely to ask questions with the present perfect tense, so it might be a good idea to prepare them for the interview session by getting them to find out specific dates and details of such things as completion of studies, moves, places visited, marriage, birth of children and so on.

Injury

Level   Intermediate and above

Time   30-40 min.

Grammar structures   Interrogatives, all tenses

In class

1   Get the students to give a definition of the word 'injure'. If necessary, consult a dictionary and write all forms of the word on the blackboard — to injure, to be injured, injury, injuries, injurious, uninjured.

2   Tell the students to write 10-15 questions they could ask another student using the word (or a form of the word) 'injure' and trying to make every question as different as possible.

3   Pair the students and ask them to answer each other's questions. Tell them to make a note in writing of any answers which they find particularly striking.

4   Each student reports to the group the most interesting answer they heard.

Other words that have also worked well in our groups:

upset, damage, expose

I'm a chair

Level   Intermediate

Time   30-40 min.

Grammar structures   Interrogatives, all tenses

In class

1   Ask a few of the students to describe their favourite armchair in size, shape, colour, age etc.

2   Tell the students they are an armchair — as an armchair, ask them to write twenty questions addressed to their favourite armchair about its experiences, e.g.:

What do you most dislike about being an armchair? Are your springs good? etc ...

Ask them to leave room for an answer under each of their questions.

3   Collect the papers in, shuffle them and give them out again, making sure nobody gets their own.

4   The students answer the questions, as armchairs.

5   Hang the papers on the walls so that people can go round and read the armchair dialogues.

NB   *In step 2 it is important to insist that as many people as possible do write a full 20 questions. The last 10 questions tend to be more interesting and imaginative than the first 10, and so provoke answers that go beyond a bald yes or no.*

I ask myself

Level   Elementary and above

Time   60-90 min.

Grammar structures   Interrogatives, all tenses

In class

1   Tell each student to write 20 questions addressed to themselves. The answers
to these questions should be of interest to another person. So, for example, a
person called Mario might start off like this:

— Mario, how old are you?
— Is your age important to you?

In *his* case the answers to the questions would be of interest to another person.

If Mario wrote:

— How many toes have you got, Mario?

This would be a bad question because in *his* case the answer is simply 10. It
could be a good question, though, if put to themselves by a person who had
lost a toe in an accident. The answer would therefore be interesting and have
some point.

2   Pair the students. Student A in each pair now addresses the questions s/he has
written to Student B. Student B replies. Student A may have to modify
slightly some of the questions on the page. If Student A has written, 'Would
you make a good husband?' and Student B is female, A will have to ask,
'Would you make a good wife?'

When A has asked all 20 questions and B has answered them, B asks A all
his/her questions.

3   Ask the students, as they finish, to find new partners and repeat the
questioning process. It feels satisfying to have worked with about 3 partners.

The reason you initially ask students to write as many as 20 questions is that it is
quite hard to produce 20 trivial ones!

Variation

Do Step 1 as above. Pair the students. A asks B his/her questions. *But B replies as s/he would expect A to.* A then tells B what his/her reply would have been.

The same is then done with B asking his/her questions and A replying in B's shoes.

Acknowledgement

We first learnt this technique from Carlos Maeztu. It is also outlined in Moskowitz (1978).

Don't use old questions

Level   Elementary and above

Time   20 min.

Grammar structures   Interrogatives

In class

1   Divide your class up into groups of 8 or 9. Have the groups of 8 or 9 milling in different parts of the room.

2   Ask each student to take a partner and ask them *two* questions about their house. The interviewer is to note down the replies. The students change partners within their groups and ask their new partner 2 *new* house questions. This process goes on until everybody has interviewed every other person in their group.
Check that the students do take notes of what their partners tell them and that they note down their partners' names.

3   Get the groups of 8 or so students sitting, if possible in a circle. They all report on the house of one person in the group. This continues until all the houses of people in the group have been reported on. The reporting within the various groups of 8 goes on simultaneously.

Acknowledgement

Jean Cureau taught us this technique at a seminar at the British Council in Paris.

Reporting as another

Level   Elementary and above

Time   20-30 min.

Grammar structures   Past simple interrogative and *Did you use to ...?*
Past simple and *I used to/I used not to.*

In class

1   Pair the students. Ask each student to interview their partner about a given
year in their life. With a group of late teenagers and young adults, we asked
people to work on their sixteenth year. Tell the interviewers to take careful
notes of what their partners tell them.

2   Ask the pairs to get together in groups of 6 (3 pairs). The groups of 6 now
work simultaneously and autonomously. In each group, one student starts off
by saying: I am ... (partner's name). They then give all the partner's
information about the year in question, but in the first person. Each person in
the sub-group then reports on their partner's year, as if they *were* the partner.

Rationale

The role-reversed reporting makes people listen much more intently — sometimes
the role-reversal gives rise to incongruous and humorous statements. The students
are learning more about each other, but in a kind of distorting, enriching mirror.

Acknowledgement

We learnt this technique from Leveton (1977).

III
Tenses

Seasons

Level   Elementary

Time   20 min.

Structure   Present simple + 'I like best'

In class

1   Write the 4 seasons as headings on the board.

2   Ask the students to close their eyes and think about one season.

3   After 2 or 3 minutes invite the students to come and write any idea or association they have with that season. If necessary they will have to explain it to the class.

4   When all the ideas have been collected and talked about ask the students to write a few sentences beginning:

The season I like best is . . . because . . .

and

The season I like least is . . . because . . .

5   As the students finish pin up their sentences and encourage them to wander round reading what the others have written.

I feel

Level   Intermediate

Time   20 min.

Structure   Present simple

Preparation

Bring in 6 large sheets of paper with one sentence on each sheet:

- I feel frightened when . . .
- I feel nervous when . . .
- I feel relaxed when . . .
- I feel uncomfortable when . . .
- I feel under stress when . .
- I feel glad when . . .

In class

1   Pin up the papers round the room and get the students to complete the statements in any way they like. Each student should try to write at least 4 statements.

2   When the papers are fairly full ask the students to sit in 6 groups.

3   Give each group a sheet to read and comment on why the students feel as they do.

4   Ask somebody from each group to report back to the whole class the most interesting points from the group discussion.

Classmates crosswords

Level   Elementary and above.

Time   20-30 min.

Structure   Present simple (the exercise could be used to focus on relative clauses)

In class

1   Ask the students to each choose 5 people from the class and put their names in the form of a grid, e.g.:

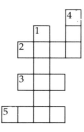

They should not show their neighbour who they have chosen.

2   On a separate sheet of paper they draw the grid without letters and write crossword-type clues, e.g.:

1-down – The girl who always comes late
2-across – The lady with long black hair
3-across – The young man who smiles a lot, etc.

This part of the exercise could be done as homework.

3   They exchange crosswords with a partner and solve them individually.

Variation

Instead of using the names of students in the class, grids may be made taking any vocabulary items the students choose to revise.

Photo families

Level   Elementary

Time   20 min.

Structure   Present simple

Preparation

Ask the students to bring in a photo of a friend or member of the family. Try to encourage them to bring photos showing people of all ages.

In class

1   Check that the students know words for members of the family, e.g. mother-in-law, niece, great-aunt, etc.

2   Put the students in groups of 8 to 10 and ask them to create a family using the photographs they have brought in.

3   They arrange the photos in a family tree and present it to other groups.

Where do you live?

Level   Beginners to elementary

Time   10 min.

Grammar structures   Present simple

In class

1   Draw the following diagram on the board:

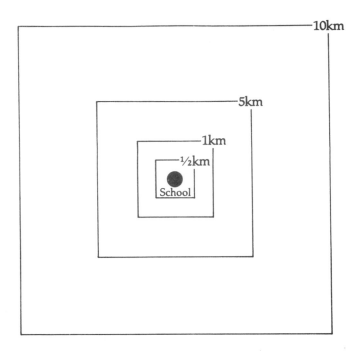

2   Divide the students into 5 groups:

Group A must find all the students that live within ½km of the school.
Group B must find all the students that live between ½km and 1km from the school.
Group C : 1km to 5km.
Group D : 5km to 10km.
Group E : over 10km.

(You will need to vary the distances to take account of your class's particular living distribution.)

3   Give the students these patterns:

Where do you live?
How far is that from here?
How long does it take you to get from home to school?

The students get up, move about the room and ask each other these questions, making notes on those classmates that live within the zone you have designated.

4   One student from each group then puts the names and travel times of the students on their list up on the board in the right place on the diagram. Encourage other people from the particular group to supply any missing names. Make sure that no-one is left out.

What do you need them for?

Level   Elementary and above

Time   10 min.

Grammar structures   Present simple interrogative, declarative and negative

In class

Tell the group you have something or some things in mind. They are to try and discover what you have in mind by repeatedly asking you the same question, for example, 'What do you need it/them for?' You give as varied and as interest-provoking answers as possible. When the students feel they have enough clues they may try and suggest what they think the thing or things are.

Often the students, having discovered what it was you had in mind, want to go back over those of your answers which they found puzzling.

This is how this exercise went in one particular lower intermediate group:

Student 1:   What do you need them for?
Teacher: For my health.

Student 2:   What do you need them for?
Teacher: Well, I find them rather beautiful ... *You* might not ...

Student 3:   What do you need them for?
Teacher: In a funny way I find that they link me, join me, with my father.

Student 4:   What do you need them for?
Teacher: Well, they annoy my wife quite a lot.

Student 5:   What do you need them for?
Teacher: Financially, from a money point of view, I don't *need* them — I could quite well do without them.
Student 6:   What do you need them for?
Teacher: They make me aware of the weather.
Student 7:   What do you need them for?
Teacher: They take less work than other things, etc ...

When the students, in this particular case, discovered that what the teacher had in mind was *potatoes*, they wanted further explanations of some of his answers!

Variation

Once you have done the exercise with the whole group focussed on you, you can ask individuals to come with things in mind *and* with a question they would like the group to repeatedly put to them. Make sure they understand that the interest of the exercise will depend on how thought-provoking their replies are.

The range of items and suitable 'insistence' questions is vast, e.g.:

Love   Where does it belong?
Old age   What do people do about it?

Acknowledgement

This exercise type grew out of ideas proposed by Richard Baudins, Dierk Andresen and Sabine Conelieson.

Drawing a friend

Level   Elementary and above

Time   30-40 min.

Grammar structures   Present simple interrogative

In class

1   Lead in by describing someone in the group in some detail — jot down some of the vocabulary you use on the board.

2   Split the class up into groups of 5. In each group, one student chooses someone they *know* well without telling the other 4 students who it is. It is better if they choose someone the classmates will not know. The 4 classmates in each group have to draw a full-length portrait of the person in the fifth student's mind. They ask the fifth student yes/no questions like: 'Does s/he have a long nose?'; 'Does s/he wear a hat?'. The student on the hot seat may only reply *yes* or *no*.

3   The person being questioned looks at their classmates' drawings and tells them where they have gone wrong.

4   Repeat steps 2 and 3 with different students in the hot seat.

How often do we do it?

Level   Elementary to intermediate

Time   15 min.

Grammar structures   Present simple, interrogative + 'do' (auxiliary) in
questions, expressions of frequency

In class

1   Put these lists up on the board:

buy — a magazine	borrow — money	see — grandparents
— a book	— pens	— boxing on TV
— a lipstick	— a ruler	— closest friend
— a pair of shoes	— a bike	— a film in a cinema
— stamps	— ideas	— boy/girl friend
— hi-fi equipment	— clothes	— a film on video
	— school books	

2   Start asking the class questions like:

How often do you go swimming?
How often do you go to church?
How often do you remember your dreams?

Encourage precise answers like: Twice a week
                                                 Once a fortnight
                                                 Every couple of months

rather than just 'often' or 'not often'.

3   Pair the students. Tell the students to find out how often their partner
buys/borrows/sees the things in the lists on the board. Go round and supply
extra frequency words or phrases that are needed. Tell the students to take
note of their partner's answers.

4   Call the students back together and ask them to guess how often a certain
person does a certain thing. You simply say the name of the student and point
to an item on the board. The group has to guess how frequently the person
named does the thing pointed at. The person's partner then confirms or denies
and corrects it.

House plans

Level   Intermediate and above

Time   40-50 min.

Grammar structures   Present simple + spatial prepositions

In class

1   Make sure the class are familiar with some of the more complex spatial
    prepositional phrases like:

    parallel to
    opposite
    diagonally opposite
    just behind
    over the ... from
    next to ... (etc)

2   Sit with your back to the board and have a student ask you questions about,
    and draw, the ground plan of your house/flat on the board as best they can.
    This gives the students a language model for what follows.

3   Ask the students to sit back to back in pairs. Student A has pen and paper
    and asks B questions about their house/flat, so that A can draw B's ground
    plan. Student B must not at this stage look at A's drawing.

4   Tell all the Bs to look at their partners' drawings and tell them where they
    have gone wrong.

5   B now questions A in an attempt to accurately draw the ground plan of A's
    house or flat. A criticises B's drawing.

NB   *This exercise works best if people who do not visit each other's flats or houses work
together.*

Imagine their living-room

Level   Elementary and above

Time   20-30 min.

Grammar structures   Present simple, there is/are

In class

1   This exercise pre-supposes your having done work with the group on words needed to describe a living-room.

Ask each student to write their name on a slip of paper. Collect the slips, shuffle them and re-distribute them, making sure no one gets their own name.

2   Tell each student to draw a plan of how they imagine or recall the living-room of the person whose name they have taken.

3   One student is asked to describe in detail the room they have drawn, mentioning position of objects, colour, style and materials. The rest of the group have to try and guess whose room has been described. The student then tells whose living-room they were thinking of. The student whose living-room it is corrects the things that the describing student got wrong.

4   Before asking other students to repeat step 3, supply the group with any vocabulary that you feel the first 2 students were short of.

5   Have other students repeat step 3.

Writing as another

Level Intermediate

Time 40 min.

Structure Past simple

In class

1 Put the students into groups of 4 and then ask them to write individually a sentence about something they did in the past, for example as a child, during their last holiday, or even the previous weekend,

   e.g.: I visited friends
          I wrote poetry
          etc.

2 Tell the students to pass their paper to another member of the group.

3 Each student reads the sentence passed to her/him and underneath writes 15-20 questions about it,

   e.g.: How long did you stay with your friends?
          Did you eat with them?
          etc.

4 Ask the students to pass the paper to another member of the group and s/he then responds to the questions, inventing the answers.

5 The 15-20 questions and answers are passed on a third time and the task is now to write a short passage using the information from the questions and answers.

6 Ask the students to pass the passage back to the writers of the original sentences. They read them and comment on how near the passage is to the original experience.

Me before

Level   Intermediate

Time   15 min.

Structure   Past simple, declarative and interrogative

In class

1   Ask the students to write 5 things on a piece of paper that they did between the ages of 18 and 25.

2   Collect all the papers and re-distribute them making sure that nobody gets her/his own.

3   Ask the students to mill. They ask each other questions about the statements they have in order to find the writer.

4   When the students have found the owner of the paper they can talk to each other long and fill in any details or give further information as they wish.

Variation

If you are teaching younger people (under 25) either get them to write about an earlier time in their life, e.g. from 5-10, or write statements about a weekend or holiday.

Demonstrations

Level   Intermediate

Time   30 min.

Structure   Past simple

In class

1   Provide a sheet prepared in the following way:

WHEN	WHERE	WHY

and ask the students if they have ever taken part in a demonstration.

2   Circulate the paper and the students can make entries.

3   Put the students into small groups taking care that each group has at least one student with a demonstration story to tell.

4   Let the students tell their story.

Variation

Adapt this activity to suit any other event, e.g. meeting a celebrity, experiencing a natural disaster, attending a national festival etc.

Accidental writing

Level   Elementary and above

Time   20-30 min.

Structure   Past simple

In class

1   Tell the students about an accident you have had – maybe as a child. Ask them to write down 5-10 key words from your story and then collect all the words on the board.

2   Ask the students to think of an accident they have had and write down just the key words (5-10) from that incident.

3   Pair the students and tell them to exchange papers (key words). The key words then become their own and they write an account of the accident in the first person singular as though it had happened to them.

4   While the students are writing you can circulate helping with vocabulary and structures where needed.

5   When the students have finished they exchange the papers, read the accounts and tell their partner how near the truth it is.

Opposites

Level   Elementary and above

Time   40-50 min.

Grammar structures   Past simple

In class

1   Ask the students to write down the 'opposites' of these words:
    good   typing   real   angry   Monday

2   Ask the students to suggest the 'opposites' they have come up with. Jot down
    the various acceptable 'opposites' on the board.
    Good has produced: *naughty, evil, bad, nasty.*

    Typing has produced: *hand-writing, reading, walking* (in that typing is a kind
    of walking with the fingers), *silent writing* etc.

    Get students to explain why they propose a given word as the opposite of one
    on the list.

3   Write the following scene up on the board and ask the students to write its
    opposite or *reversal*. Don't give examples of how to do this as, if you do, this
    will reduce the diversity of the students' reactions to the task.

    The waitress came up to Table No. 3 and offered the tall man the menu. He
    chose and ordered. She went back to the kitchen to get what he wanted.

    Confronted with this task, some students simply put all the sentences into the
    negative. Others try to find 'opposites' and write:

    'A waiter went down to chair letter C and took away the bill from the short
    woman.'

4   Group the students in fours to read their 'reversals' to one another.

5   Now tell the students that your are going to tell them the reversal of a bad
    experience from your own life. We once told this story in class:

    'I went to work as an au pair in France. It was a marvellous family with very
    few children. My hostess was very kind and understanding. I had almost no

work to do and oceans of free time. I had been going to stay for 2 weeks, but in the end I stayed for 6 months.'

6   Ask the students to shut their eyes and think of some bad experience they have had. Also ask them to prepare to tell the experience to someone else, but reversed.

7   Find out how many people have brought back bad experiences to mind, group them with people who haven't and ask them to tell their reversed stories.

8   Ask the listeners to now tell the stories they have heard to others in the group, and so on.

Rationale

At first sight, the exercise above may seem a little strange, but it provokes very strong listening comprehension, as the listener is doing a double decoding: i) s/he is making sense of the sounds and words of the L2; and ii) s/he is trying to 'reverse' the scene being listened to, to find the real meaning.

Variation

Instead of bringing sad situations to mind and telling them happily, you could ask the students to bring back happy situations and tell them sadly.

All sorts of opposites can be played, e.g. with: trivial/important
                                                    recent/far back in time
                                                    selfless/boasting.

Acknowledgement

This exercise type comes from the work of Fritz Perls in Gestalt therapy. An excellent source for Gestalt therapy exercises is Stevens (1971).

Running away

Level Elementary and above

Time 30–40 min.

Grammar structures Past simple

In class

1 Explain to the class that you are going to give them a theme and ask them to react to the theme by saying any words that they associate with it. Ask for a volunteer to come and write the words the group produce on the board. Tell the volunteer to write the words in *disorder* all over the board.

2 When the volunteer is up by the board with chalk or pen at the ready, yourself write up the theme:

RUNNING AWAY FROM HOME

The students fire their associations at the volunteer in the form of words or phrases. The board may end up looking like this:

Some students will know the word they want to shout out, but only in the mother tongue. Help them with a translation. Stop the brain-storming when there are 30–40 words up on the board.

3 Have the students work in groups of 3 and put the words that are in disorder on the board into idea-groups or categories. Each of their categories must have a heading.

4 Ask the students if any of them ever *wanted to*, *tried to* or *actually* ran away from home when they were younger. In our testing of these techniques we found that around half of most groups had either wanted to, tried to or actually run away from home.

5 Have the 'runners away' tell their stories simultaneously to others in small groups, depending for size on the number of students in the class and on the numbers of 'runners away'.

Danger

This exercise can have an inhibiting effect on a group if people don't yet know each other reasonably well.

Things I have owned

Level   Elementary and above

Time   20 min.

Grammar structures   Past simple

In class

1 Ask each student to choose a class of things they own and have owned for some time, e.g.: watches, pets, jewellery, handbags, bikes, cars. Tell them the class they choose ought to consist of things that are important to them.

2 Ask them to write down all the things they have owned in the category they have chosen, the year they got each one, what it looked like, its colour etc. — a full description.

3 Put the students in small groups to discuss how they felt when they got each thing, how it was important to them and if their relationship to it would be, or is, the same today.

Variation

If you know that all your students own bikes and see them as important possessions you could ask them all to work round bikes they have owned; the same with cars, jewels etc.

A thing I stole

Level   Elementary and above

Time   40 min.

Grammar structures   Past simple

Preparation

Make copies of the children's rhyme below so that everybody can be given one. Prepare to tell the story of some theft of yours in the past, that you feel you can share with the group.

In class

1   Give out copies of *Cookie Jar.*

- *Who stole the cookie from the cookie jar, was it you Number .....?*
- *Who me?*
- *Yes you!*
- *Couldn't be!*
- *Then who?*
- *Number .....!*

2   Make sure everybody understands the words in the rhyme. Number the class off, so that each person has a number and is clear what it is.

Start the ball rolling by yourself chanting the first 2 lines of rhyme and rhythmically clapping. Make sure you emphasise the syllables on which the stress falls. The student whose number you have called replies, in rhythm, *Who me?* and you continue the dialogue with the student, who in the last line calls another number. The student then becomes the accuser and starts the rhyme again with the new number as the accused, and so on.

Keep a good rhythm going and don't let the pace drag; have everyone clapping in time.

3   Change the mood in the room by quietly beginning to tell the story of when you stole something.

4   Ask everybody to try and think of a stealing story of their own that they feel able to tell. If your class is early teenagers make it clear that you don't want any theft stories that are less than 3 years old! It helps to bring stories back to mind if people shut their eyes.

5   Find out how many story-tellers you have in the group. Group these with the people who can't or don't want to tell a story. Tell them to listen as carefully as possible to the 'thieves' stories.

6   Ask the listeners to work with new people and tell the stories they have heard, and so on, until the stories told have got round the group.

Danger

You should not use this exercise until people know each other quite well, as people who don't want to tell theft stories may feel pressurised into telling them simply because others have.

You should steer completely clear of this technique if you happen to be teaching ESP groups among whom large-scale theft is professionally normal!

Rationale

If people are going to get to know each other via L2 on a language course it is important that they get to know them a bit for real. We do not agree with Gertrude Moskowitz's feeling that awareness activities should perpetually emphasise the positive in people. Since light only exists in contrast to shade, we feel that there should be some careful exploration of the shade.

Classes in which we have used this stealing exercise have invariably got to know one another better, as the shock of speaking about this area has a loosening-up effect. The linguistic spin-off is that the L2 is being used to convey something important to which the listener is really listening. This kind of exercise endows the L2 with affective reality.

Is it true?

Level   Elementary and above

Time   10-15 min. in the first class and 15-30 min. in the second and subsequent classes

Grammar   Past simple

Preparation

Prepare to tell a story about yourself that is either 100% true or 100% false. If it is true, tell it so it feels wrong — leave things out, hesitate a little in the telling, exude the feeling that you are lying. If it is false, tell it as realistically and as calmly and matter-of-factly as possible. To practise telling the story to the class, mumble it to yourself first.

In class

1   Explain to the students that you are going to tell them a story that is either 100% true or 100% false. Their task is to listen to you and to watch you and decide which it is. Tell them you will not mix false and true elements.

2   Tell the story.

3   Tell the students they may each ask one 'detective' question about the story. The only question that may not be asked is 'Was it true?' If a student has more than one question to ask, they should whisper it to a classmate who has not yet asked a question and have it asked by them.

4   Put the students in fours to discuss whether they think you were lying or truth telling. Don't walk round listening — you will inhibit discussion if you do. If this stage of the lesson slips back into the mother tongue, too bad.

5   Ask the students to vote on whether they think you were lying or not.

6   Finally, tell them the truth.

7   As homework, ask them to prepare to tell a similar sort of story, either 100% true or 100% false, in the next class. Tell them to prepare to tell it by mumbling it through to themselves, *not* by writing it out.

In the next class

1   Not all students will be ready to tell a story. Divide the class in 2 and have one story-teller in each half. Have the 2 halves working simultaneously, with each of the 2 students doing exactly as you did in the previous lesson (steps 2-6). Repeat in both groups with two more story-tellers.

2   You will probably still have plenty of people with prepared stories left over. Use them in subsequent lessons through the term. This exercise frame can be used over and over again as people's skill at and interest in lying is close to inexhaustible.

Acknowledgement

We learnt this technique from Joan Hewitt's presentation of it in Sion (1980).

Damaged property

Level   Intermediate and above

Time   30 min.

Grammar structures   Past simple

Preparation

Find an object you own that is damaged.

In class

1   Show the students your damaged object and let them speculate how they think the damage happened.

2   Tell the students to think of an object they own that is damaged or that was damaged and to list 10 adjectives and adverbs describing how they felt and reacted when it was damaged. Tell them not to name the object.

3   Pair the students and tell them to exchange lists. Each student can ask 3 'yes/no questions' to help them imagine what their partner's object is.

4   Tell each student to write a short account (80-100 words) about their partner's object (what they imagine it is) and to include how they think it got damaged and what the owner's reaction was.

5   Ask them to read their neighbour's account and then tell the 'real' story.

Who were you?

Level   Elementary and above

Time   15 min.

Grammar structures   Ago/past simple interrogative, declarative and negative

In class

1   Ask a student to come out in front of the group and repeatedly ask you the same question: 'Who were you 10 years ago?' You have to give as many different answers as you can, e.g.:

Student: Who were you 10 years ago?
You: I was a single person
Student: Who were you 10 years ago?
You: I was a student … etc.

After giving 20-30 different answers to the same question, reverse the process and put the same question repeatedly to the student.

2   Pair the students. Ask them to repeat the exercise above, with one person asking 'Who were you 10 years ago?' over and over again and the other trying to give as many diverse answers as possible.

NB   This exercise is a powerful way of getting German speakers to realise deeply that Wer *in their language becomes* Who *in English and has nothing to do with* Where.

Variation

10 years ago may or may not be the best time to get your group to focus back to, so vary the time to suit the group.

There are hundreds of other good question sentences for getting students to work on the past tense, e.g.:

What were you scared of x years ago?
What did you like x years ago?

Sitting in a group

Level Elementary and above

Time 20 min.

Grammar structures Past simple and spatial prepositions

In class

1   Ask the students to describe how the seats were arranged in the classroom when they went to primary school. Did they like the arrangement? Who decided on the particular arrangement? Where did each student like to sit? Could they choose or change their seat?

2   Tell the students to think of 4 or 5 times during the last month when they sat in a group of more than 3 people.

3   Get them to draw a plan of the seating arrangements of a couple of these occasions, not forgetting to mark where they sat.

4   Pair the students and ask them to explain to their partners why they chose or were allocated to a particular position in the group.

Remembering back

Level   Elementary and above

Time   10 min. in the first class and 15-30 min. in the second.

Grammar structures   Past simple and present simple

Preparation

Bring to mind a place you knew well when you were a small child (under 10) and which you have seen or still see as an adult. Prepare to describe it as it appeared to you then as a child (past tense) and as you see it now (present tense).

In class

1   Explain to the class that you are going to describe a place you knew well as a child, as you saw it then. Describe the place (not more than 2 min.). Pause to see if students want to elicit more information by questioning you.

2   Describe the same place as you see it now.

3   For homework, ask the students to each come to the next class with 2 similar descriptions prepared. Tell them not to write their parallel descriptions but to get them fluent by composing them mentally and then mumbling them to themselves.

In the next class

Group the students in fours to produce their parallel descriptions. Remind them to use the past simple in the first description and the present simple in the second.

A teacher I disliked

Level   Elementary and above

Time   50-60 min.

Grammar structures   Present simple and past simple

In class

1   Ask the students to close their eyes and bring their secondary schools back to mind. Help them to do this by reading the sentences below with long pauses between them — read in a slow, contemplative voice:

●   I can see the entry to the school ...
(Pause)
●   I notice the area outside the school, the colours, the shapes ...
(Pause)
●   I go into the school — I can hear sounds and see faces ...
(Pause)
●   I go into one of my classrooms — I remember how the place smelled, the way the light fell on the desks, the colours...

2   Ask a few of the students to give three or four sentence descriptions of what their schools were like.

3   Ask the students to close their eyes again and think back to the teacher at secondary school they most disliked. Invite them especially to think back to how this teacher actually walked into class and started a typical lesson.

4   Ask for a volunteer to *mime* their most disliked teacher coming into the classroom and starting a lesson. The person miming should get together any props they need (e.g. book, bag, cigarette etc.). They should leave the room and make a real entry. Before the volunteer starts the action, ask them if the students need to sit differently to make the scene more realistic and if they need to get up when s/he enters as the most disliked teacher.

   The mime, from the volunteer's entry, should not last more than 2 min.

5   As soon as the mime finishes, ask the volunteer to sit down in front of the group and stay in role as the disliked teacher. Tell the group to write 5 or 6 questions they would like to put to the teacher they have just seen mimed. They are to write as peers of the teacher, not as his/her pupils.

6   The students fire their questions at the volunteer, who replies as much as possible in character.

7   Many people in the group will have strong memories of their own most disliked teacher which have not yet been directly dealt with in the exercise. Ask each person to close their eyes and imagine a meeting, today, with the teacher in question. Ask them to write down *in one sentence* what they would say to him/her to sum up their feeling.

8   Have everybody up and moving round the room, saying their sentences to each other. When students hear sentences that intrigue them, they ask the other person to explain further.

Danger

We do not recommend that this exercise be done with students at secondary school, as most disliked teachers could then well be your own colleagues!

Acknowledgement

This exercise is in the psychodrama tradition and we have to thank Bernard Dufeu and Marcia Karp for our introduction to psychodrama techniques.

Things they did

Level   Elementary and above

Time   30–40 min.

Grammar structures   Present simple to past simple — focus on irregular verbs

In class

1   Put these 2 circles of verbs on the board and check the students know all the meanings:

A   B

keeps finds   throws lends
       learns   shoots
brings   wins   tells   swears

buys   steals says   sends
     gets eats catches sells   teaches
                             gives

2   Tell the students there are 2 people: Person A does the things in the first circle and Person B does the things in the second circle. Ask each student to choose to work with either Person A or Person B and then to write:

a) the person's name
b) the person's favourite colour
c) 5 things the person normally does on Sunday
d) a story in the past tense including all the actions in the person's circle.

3   Group the students in fours and have them read out what they have written to each other.

Variation

All the verbs in the A circle above are to do with *receiving* or *taking*, while the B set of verbs are *getting rid of* or *giving* actions. You could use the same exercise frame with another pair of psychological set of irregular verbs, e.g.:

Aggressive   *Contemplative*

burn   know
cut   think   dream
catch
lead   choose   lean
strike
forbid   misunderstand   withdraw
bite   see   become
begin
overcome
sell

Hiding preferences

Level   Elementary and above

Time   20-40 min.

Grammar structures   Present simple, mainly 3rd person; past simple

In class

1   Put this list up on the board:

2 places
2 people
2 meals
2 books
2 houses
2 girls
2 men
2 cars
2 pictures
2 pieces of music

2   Choose one pair yourself from the list above. Suppose you have chosen 2 places, the first item on the list, silently think of a place you very much like and one you very much dislike. Tell the class you are going to describe 2 places to them and that they are to decide which one you like and which one you dislike.

Now describe the 2 places to the class, *doing your best not to reveal your own preference.* One place could be a past place and one a present one.

3   Group the students in fours and ask them to decide which place you like and which you dislike. The fours report to the whole group. You ask the class to vote. Finally you tell them the truth!

4   Divide the students into groups of 8-10 and re-run the exercise with a student in the hot seat in each group.

Fantasy at a window

Level   Post-beginner to lower intermediate

Time   10-20 min.

Grammar structures   Present continuous, declarative, interrogative and negative

In class

1   Put these patterns up on the board:

What can you see now?

Is she/he
Are they } . . . ing?

What is she/he
       are they doing now?

etc. . . .

2   Go to the window, look out and describe something imaginary happening out there. After 3 or 4 sentences of present continuous action description, pause and elicit questions from the group. Continue your description guided by their questions.

3   Have an able student take over from you at the window. She/he starts a new commentary on imaginary actions. You help her/him with language.

Comparing people

Level   Elementary

Time   10-15 min.

Structure   Present simple and continuous

Preparation
Bring lots of magazine pictures of people.

In class
1   Ask the students in groups of about 4 to describe the appearance of a person of their choice – member of the family or a friend.

2   When each student in the group has described her/his person, give the group a stack of magazine pictures.

3   The students look through the pictures and choose the picture they think best matches the description they have heard.

4   The students then say why or why not the chosen picture matches her/his person.

Variation
The students can be asked previously to bring in a photo of their 'person', which can then be used as comparison with the chosen magazine picture at the end.

At the time of the photo

Level   Elementary and above

Time   15 min.

Grammar structures   Past continuous, past simple, past perfect

Preparation

Ask the students to bring in a photo of themselves and bring one yourself.

In class

1   Show your own photo and say:

what you *were doing* when the photo was taken,
what you *had* just *done* before it was taken,
what you *did* immediately after.

2   Ask the students to write the 3 sentences in the same way about their photos, but not to show the photo to anybody else.

3   The students put the sentences up round the wall.

4   Collect the photos and distribute them so that nobody gets his or her own.

5   The students must then walk round and read the pinned-up sentences and match their photo to the appropriate sentences.

The weekend

Level   Elementary and above

Time   20-30 min.

Grammar structures   Past simple, past continuous

Preparation

Bring in a large sheet of paper and a felt-tipped pen per student, if possible, and Blu-tack to hang pictures on the wall.

In class

1   On the blackboard, draw a pin-person diagram of how you spent the weekend, e.g.:

Give a 2-minute explanation of the diagram. Allow time for students to ask you questions if they feel like doing this.

2   Give out the sheets and felt pens. Ask each student to draw pictures of their weekend. Make it clear that what usually happens can be as interesting as what only occasionally happens.

3   Group the students in eights near a wall. Get one student in each group to hang their pictures on the wall and to describe their weekend using the pictures as visual aids. Keep a check on students' use of the past tenses.

4   Have each student in each group take the hot seat in their group and repeat step 3.

5   Write up the following on the board and make sure all the meanings are clear:

a rest	a new experience
an escape	an exciting experience
a beginning	a failure
a bore	a deepening experience
a continuation	
a success	
a shock	
an end	

If any of the above fit your weekend explain to the class why. Ask students to comment about their weekends and explain if any of the suggestions on the board are relevant to their weekends.

Dates

Level   Elementary and above

Time   20 min.

Grammar structures   Past simple, past continuous

In class

1   Tell the students a precise date in the last 5 years when something important happened to you. Get them all to write it down. Now tell them what it was that happened to you. Ask them:

'What were *you* doing on the xth of y, 19..?'

As far as possible, have them give past continuous answers, though some students may need to say things like: 'I had just xed the day before that.' Don't disallow these needs.

2   Group the students in eights and ask each person to think of a precise date on which something important happened to them in the last 5 years. It must be a date they can talk about to others. If your students are adults you might offer them a longer period than 5 years.

3   Ask student A in each sub-group to read out their date to the rest, who write it down. A then tells the story of what happened on that day. The other students in the group then say: "On ... I was ...ing." You will need to go round and feed in phrases like:

I think I was ...
I was probably ...
I should think I was ...
Perhaps I was ...

Each student tells story of their date.

Focusing in on the past

Level   Intermediate

Time   20-30 min.

Grammar structures   Present perfect, past simple

Preparation

Bring in enough slips of paper (one for each student) prepared with one present perfect structure, e.g.:

_____   has written to a newspaper
_____   has been fined for speeding
_____   has met a famous person
_____   has had a confrontation with the police or the authorities
_____   has been on the radio
_____   has slept on a mountain
_____   has been in hospital for a long time
_____   has written poetry

The statements chosen should neither be too way-out nor refer to 'normal' everyday activities.

In class

1   Give each student a slip of paper and tell them to mill asking the question 'Have you ever . . . ?'
    If they get a positive answer they are to fill in the name of the people in the gap, but not to collect any more information.

2   The students sit in a circle and one of them begins by reading out one sentence, e.g.:

    Anna has met a famous person

    and that student is then invited to tell the details to the whole group (which requires the past tense).

3   The exercise can last up to 30 minutes as the students are normally quite interested to hear the stories.

Circle games 1

Level   Post-beginner to elementary

Time   10-15 min.

Grammar structures   Present perfect simple, relative clauses, I want +
infinitive

In class

Seat yourself and the students in a circle. You need to have one empty chair next to
you. If you can't get the chairs in a circle (because, say, you have benches screwed to
the floor) have the students stand in a circle and have a big space between you and
the person to your right.

Say to the group: 'I want someone who has had a nightmare recently to come and sit
next to me' (any experience that someone in the group is likely to have had will fit the
bill here). If someone *has* had a recent nightmare they come and sit next to you. This
vacates a chair somewhere else in the circle. A student on either side of the empty
chair invites 'someone who has X experience' to come and sit next to them. You may
want to put the pattern up on the board.

Rationale

This is an animated structure drill in which you totally control the pattern but the
students say the things they want to to each other. This type of exercise wakes a tired
group up and allows controlled movement.

Circle games 2

Level   Post-beginner to elementary

Time   10-15 min.

Grammar structures   Present continuous + vocabulary of dress and colour, relative clauses, I want + infinitive

In class

As above but the students invite others to fill the empty chair by reference to dress: e.g. 'I want someone with/who is wearing/red shoes to come and sit next to me.'

Circle games 3

Level   Post-beginner to elementary

Time   10-15 min.

Grammar structures   Present continuous with future reference, relative clauses, I want + infinitive

In class

As above but with reference to the coming weekend:

'I want someone who's mountain-climbing this weekend to . . . .

NB   *You will find another 'circle' exercise for working on comparatives on page 118 of* Grammar Games, *Rinvolucri, CUP.*

Experiences I haven't had

Level Lower intermediate

Time 30-40 min.

Grammar structures Present perfect + *never* and *yet*

In class

1 Give the students these two patterns:

I've never
I haven't yet

2 Head the left hand side of board: *Good experiences I haven't had* and the right hand side of the board: *Bad experiences I haven't had*. Ask for two 'secretaries' to come and write at the board.

3 Tell the group to shout out *good* or *bad* experiences they haven't had, making full sentences. Each student should specify which category she wants her sentence to go into. For some 'I haven't got married' is left hand side, for some right hand side! Let the students fill the board with their present perfect sentences.

4 Ask half the class to work in groups of 3 rank-ordering the good experiences in order of excellence. The other half of the class works in 3s and rank-orders the other side in order of badness.

5 Ask the 3s from one half to team up with the 3s from the other half, forming groups of 6. They share and discuss their rankings. In some groups there is fierce philosophical debate along these lines: 'does not having had a good experience equate with a bad experience?'

Technical note

The ideal surface to do this exercise on is a photocopying whiteboard. You press a button and each student gets her own paper copy of what is on the board. The copier board is an intensely student-centred item of technology. Sadly, at the time of writing, not many of us have them.

What's it all about?

Level   Elementary and above

Time   20-30 min.

Grammar structures   Interrogatives; past simple, present perfect, present simple.

In class

1   Give a visual outline on the board of some significant past experience of yours. Accompany this with a minimal verbal account either on the board or spoken, thus provoking the class's desire to ask questions, e.g.:

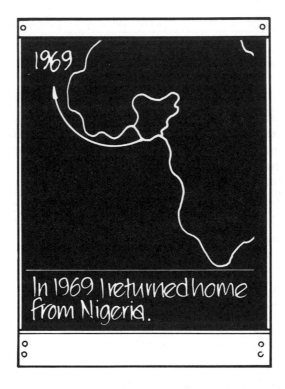

2   Invite the students to write 8-10 questions addressed to you about your experience. Tell them they can write frank questions and that you will try to reply as fully as possible. Go round helping them with words they need and checking on what they have written.

3 Sit facing the class and try to get out of your teacher role. Invite the students to question you and answer as openly and warmly as you can. Very likely the students will ask many questions beyond those they wrote down.

4 The same exercise frame can well be used in subsequent classes with volunteer students taking your place. Make sure the volunteer realises that at the beginning they must offer strong information, but not too much of it, or there will be no need for the group to ask questions.

The shortest route

Level   Elementary and above

Time   15-20 min.

Grammar structures   Present simple and future; *by* bus, *by* plane, *on* foot

In class

1 Divide the students into groups of 8. Tell them where you live. Tell them that you would like to visit each student in each group of 8. Ask each 8 to plan the best possible route for you to visit each of them and then get back to your home. Add that you will have to take public transport as you have no car or bike. (The routes may be from country to country or from one street to the next, depending on the type of group.) To guide their discussion, give them some useful patterns on the board:

S/he takes the bus from A to B.
S/he changes at…
S/he'll have to take a taxi here.
S/he takes the plane from… with a stop-over at…
S/he won't get there until… if…

As they plan your route in the groups of 8, go round listening, but do not interfere. This is an excellent diagnostic exercise.

2 Ask one group to come to the board and sketch a map of your route. Ask them each to tell you and the rest of the class how to get to their particular homes. Question each student about alternative ways of travelling.

Do not repeat this reporting with each group of 8, as this would be heavy and tedious.

Past picture

Level   Elementary and above

Time   20 min.

Grammar structures   Past simple, past continuous

Preparation

Take into class a photo of yourself when you were a lot younger.

In class

1   Show the picture to the students and comment on it. At this stage don't answer any questions.

2   Put the picture away in order to focus their attention on the past and to prevent questions using present continuous.

3   Ask the students to write 10 questions addressed to 'you now,' about 'you then'. Make it clear that questions about the time in the picture should be in the past continuous, e.g.:

What were you doing on the boat?
What colour was the shirt you were wearing?

and questions in general about you then are simple past, e.g.:

Did you always go sailing in the summer?
Did you live near the sea?

4   Invite the students to fire their questions at you. Encourage supplementary questions.

In the next class

They bring in photos of themselves and the activity is repeated in pairs.

Variation

Tell the students to each bring a photo of themselves or of a member of their family or of a friend to class for the next lesson.

In the next lesson, group the students in 4s. One student in each group holds up their photo and the other 3 question him or her about it — who, where, when, why etc...

The 3 students in each group then decide why the fourth brought *that* photo to class. Then the 'photo' student tells them in fact why s/he did. The other 3 students show their photos in turn in the same way.

Who wrote about me?

Level   Elementary and above

Time   20-30 min.

Grammar structures   3rd person singular of present simple and present continuous

Preparation

Bring Blu-tack and cards to class for students to write on.

In class

1   Ask each student to write their name on a piece of paper. Collect the papers, shuffle them and re-distribute them, making sure nobody gets their own name.

2   Give out the cards and ask each person to write one paragraph about the physical appearance and the character of the student whose name they have been given. Tell the students to write as clearly as they can on the cards, but *not* to write either their own name or the name of the person they are describing; tell them, however, that they'll have to own up eventually!

Make clear that if they are writing about the particular clothes the person is wearing today, they will need to use present continuous, but that habitual things about the person will go into the present simple, e.g.:

She's wearing red shoes.
She doesn't like sport.

3   Give out Blu-tack and ask the students to stick up what they have written round the walls of the classroom. Ask them to circulate and read the cards until they find the description that fits them. Ask them to correct the language of this card, take it to the writer (who they identify by calling out, 'Who wrote about me?') and discuss the mistakes, both grammatical and factual. If there are disagreements, invite students to present these to the whole class.

My friends' achievements

Level   Elementary and above

Time   20 min.

Grammar structures   Present perfect

In class

1   Draw a sociogram on the board showing yourself and 4 or 5 of your friends, acquaintances etc. The distance between you at the centre and your friends round you denotes the degree of closeness you feel. Under your sociogram write a present perfect sentence about each friend, e.g.:

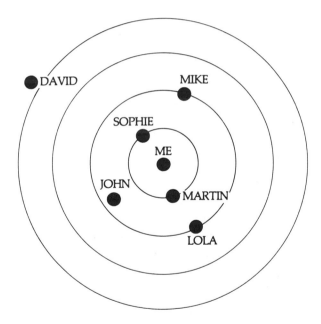

- David's at last published our book.
- John's decided to go to China for three months.
- Mike hasn't told me why he isn't fully happy at the moment.
- Sophie's got another job.
- Martin hasn't managed to change from his rather strict school to a more open one.
- Lola has just refused to do a bit of shopping for the family.

2 Ask the students to do a sociogram of themselves and 4 or 5 friends. Ask them to write a sentence for each friend about things this friend has recently achieved, failed to do, felt etc...

3 Ask the students to get up, mill, choose a partner and explain their sociograms and what they have written about the people.

A favourite place

Level   Elementary and above

Time   20-30 min.

Grammar structures   Present perfect

In class

1 Ask the students to think of a favourite place in their lives. It must be a place they have been to several times. (If they choose a place they have only been to once, the structure proposed doesn't work.)

2 Ask them to sketch a place *on the way to* their favourite place, just before they get there. Ask them to write down 5 adjectives to describe their favourite place.

3 Ask the students to complete these sentences:

- I've known this place for ...
- I've been there ... times.
- I've liked this place since ...
- I've often ... there.
- I've never ... in this place.
- I've always liked this place but ...
- I've ...

4 Get the students working in 3s comparing their sketches, adjectives and sentences; encourage them to describe their favourite place and to expand freely on the sentences they have written.

You've had it for...

Level   Elementary and above

Time   15 mins.

Grammar structures   'For and 'since' + present perfect, 'ago' + past simple

In class

1   Sit the students in straight lines facing each other. Tell them to observe the 3 people opposite them very carefully, and silently guess when they bought their clothes or other belongings or how long they've had them. Give the students a 2-minute *silent* observation period.

2   Put the following patterns up on the board:

You've probably S/he's probably I should think you've s/he's I guess you've s/he's	had	X	since... for...

I reckon you/s/he I'm pretty sure you/s/he You probably S/he probably	were/was given got bought	X	ago.

3   Get a student to make a hypothesis about the ring, shoes, beard, skirt etc., of one of the people opposite, using one of the patterns given. Other students may disagree with the first hypothesis and then finally the owner of the object or attribute will tell people how long they have had it or how long ago they got it. Repeat with many students hypothesising.

4   To round off the exercise, ask each student to tell the group which thing they've had the longest and which thing they've had the shortest time.

Acknowledgement

This exercise grew out of an observation technique we found in Spolin (1973).

Was my teacher like that?

Level   Lower intermediate and above

Time   20-30 min.

Grammar structures   Habitual past: used to, 'd, past simple + adverb of frequency

Preparation

Make sure the students come to class with two different coloured pens. Prepare a set of statements about yourself at the age of 8-10. Here are four about Mario:

- I used to read a lot
- I'd often feel angry with my father
- We went to the cinema from time to time
- I used to have loads of friends.

The first three statements are true, the last one is false. In preparing 12-14 statements about yourself at the age of ten mix true and false ones.

In class

1   Tell the class you are going to dictate some statements about yourself when you were young. Some of the statements will be true, some false. They are to write the ones they reckon are true in one colour and the false ones in the other. Give the dictation.

2   Ask the students to compare colours. They should try and justify their choices. Finally tell them which were true and which false.

Variation

Make up a set of *true* statements about yourself at a time in the past. Tell the students to write down the ones which are only true of you in one colour and the ones that are also true of them in the other.

Acknowledgement

John Morgan, author of Once Upon a Time, *suggested the idea in the variation.*

What I imagine you used to do

Level   Intermediate and above

Time   30 min.

Grammar structures   Used to/would/'d (= past habit); past simple +
adverb of frequency

In class

1   Divide your class into groups of 6-8 people. Have them sit so they can see and
hear each other.

2   Ask the students to write their names on slips of paper, fold these over and
give them to one student in each sub-group. This student shuffles them. The
others then draw a name from the pile, but it must not be their own name.

Go up to a student and say: 'You were (their real name), who are you now?'
Do this to several students until it is clear to everybody that they are going to
work within their new identity.

3   Ask each student, in their new identity, to think about the time when they
were between 5 and 10 years old, and to fill in these sentences:

●   I often used to...
●   I'd never...
●   They didn't use to let me...
●   I used to wonder...
●   I'd sometimes feel...
●   When they..., I'd...
●   They'd often make me...

4   In each sub-group, Student A says: 'I am...' (giving their new identity). 'When
I was between 5 and 10 years old I often used to...' The real student then has a
right to agree to what A has said or to disagree, e.g.: 'No, I never used to...'
Student A then reads their next sentence for the real owner of the identity to
confirm or contradict.

Roles in a masterpiece

Level　　Intermediate and above

Time　　40-50 min.

Grammar structures　　Imperative/I want you to/you are... ing/you should...

Preparation

Choose large reproductions of 2 good paintings featuring 4 or 5 figures involved together in a scene. The people's posture and gesture should be clear and unambiguous. A painting makes this exercise a lot more lively, but a magazine picture is a fair substitute.

In class

1　Ask for a volunteer who likes art and paintings. Give them a painting and tell them not to let the other students see it. Ask the volunteer to pick 4 or 5 people to represent the figures in the painting.

　Now tell the class to turn their backs to the blackboard and ask the 4 or 5 to go down to the back of the classroom. (You have to make sure there is space there for them to move in.)

2　Now ask the volunteer to tell the 4 or 5 'actor' students to take up the positions s/he can see in the painting. Don't input any language to the volunteer at this point. Tell him/her to 'sculpt' the actor students only using the voice; gesture is not allowed.

　While they are doing this, you write down on the board things that could be improved. The aim of this exercise is to enrich the range of language used by the volunteer.

3　Free the actors from their sculpture, ask the whole class to turn round and face the board, and go through the language used by the volunteer. Get the group to suggest improvements. In terms of structures, introduce all those listed above, the main ones that get used by native speakers in doing this exercise.

4　Ask for a new volunteer and have them work through the steps 1 and 2 again with a new picture and a new group of actors.

5   Go through the volunteer's language problems with the whole group. Since this exercise is quite a test of a native speaker's powers of expression, it can well be used with very advanced second language learners.

Your classroom, during the 'sculpting' phase of this exercise, might look like this:

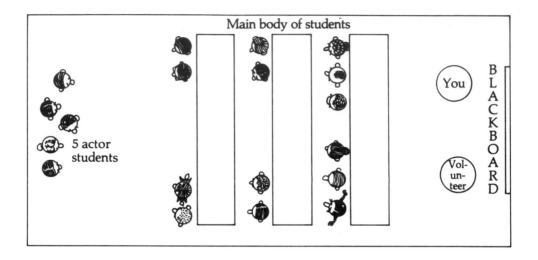

Acknowledgement

We learnt this exercise from Leveton (1977).

Future achievements

Level   Intermediate and above

Time   20-30 min.

Grammar structures   Future and future perfect tenses

Preparation

Copy the timeline opposite so you can give a copy to each student.

In class

1   Ask the students to write down 3 achievements they are pleased with.

2   Give each student a copy of the timeline and ask them to mark in below the line, the year *now* and *in 20 years time*. The sloping lines represent every second year between *now* and *20 years hence*. Ask the students to write the years in.

3   Give some examples about how *you* might fill in the timeline, thinking of possible future achievements and using some of the patterns suggested on the timeline sheet. If we were giving examples of the class, we might say:

We hope we'll have finished this book by 1984!

Hannah'll be at secondary school by 1986, etc.

4   Now ask each student to imagine what they will have achieved by every marked year on the timeline and to write a sentence for every marked year (9 sentences in all), writing up the sloping lines.

5   Group the students in 3s and ask them to compare past achievements and timelines, reading their sentences out — as you go round listening, encourage the fully contracted forms, verbally if not in writing.

TIMELINE

I'll probably've ....ed by ....
In .... I'll perhaps....
By.... I still won't've....
In .... I'll be ....ing
By.... I may've....ed....
I hope I'll have....ed by....

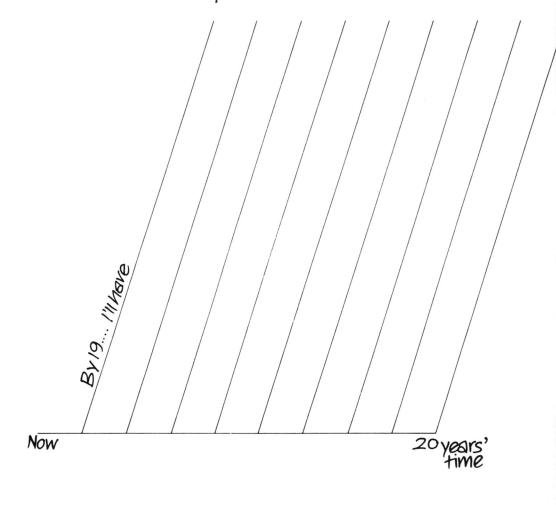

IV
Verb Forms

What she'll do if...

Level   Elementary and above

Time   10-20 min.

Grammar structures   'First' conditional

In class

1   Pair the students. Ask the pairs to work simultaneously and think up 5 actions
    A might *mime* doing to B and 5 actions B could *mime* doing to A. To get the
    students thinking, give some examples:

    A pats B's hand
    B stares at A
    A ignores B
    B kisses A, etc.

    Go round supplying vocabulary the students will need.

2   Get a volunteer pair out in front of the class. Ask A to start miming one of the
    actions but to *freeze* the action halfway through. At this point invite
    comments from the class about B's likely reaction, using this pattern:

    If A slaps B's face, B'll...

    Let B tell the group what s/he'll do if A finishes his/her action!

3   Repeat step 2 with several pairs but only let each pair do 4 or 5 of their
    actions. Ask later pairs to try and avoid actions that have already been mimed
    before. Keep the pace brisk.

If I were you, I'd . . .

Level   Elementary and above

Time   20-30 min.

Grammar structures   'Second' conditional

Preparation

Bring in one or two letters from the 'agony column' of a magazine.

In class

1   Read the letters and answers and discuss the sort of problems that are normally published in such a column.

2   Brainstorm other problem areas that come up from day to day and list the sort of people that are asked to help solve problems.

3   Ask the students to think of a problem they have to solve or have had to solve and write it on a piece of paper.

4   Collect the slips of paper and redistribute them so that nobody gets his or her own.

5   Write on the board:

    If I were you I'd . . .

    and draw the students' attention to the fact that this structure is often used when giving advice.

6   Tell the students to mill and to tell another student the problem from his paper as if it was his own. The listener gives some advice, tell his/her problem and in turn receives advice.

7   The students then exchange problems and go off and find a new partner to ask for and give advice to.

8   This procedure is repeated several times.

9   Ask the class to return to their seats and select some of the problems at random. Let the students recall advice they received for dealing with these problems.

A conditional questionnaire

Level   Upper intermediate

Time   30 min.

Grammar structures   'Second' conditional (unreal conditions)

Preparation

Bring in copies (one for each student) of a psychology questionnaire, e.g. on *Fear*.

In class

1   Brainstorm *Fear* and collect the words/ideas in a random fashion on the board.

2   Get the students to put the words/ideas into 3 to 5 groups. They may do this individually in their exercise books or it may immediately be done on the board with the whole group. (Through this categorization the students can find themselves that there are sources of fear such as persons, things and situations and individual reactions.)

3   Distribute the copies and ask the students to study the questions. Help with the vocabulary if needed.

4   Tell the students to cross out those questions they see as irrelevant or they do not want to answer. They then copy about 5 questions they rate most important onto a piece of paper.

5   They mill asking their questions and marking the answers (+) and (−) on their papers.

6   They give a statistical breakdown of their interviews using quantifiers such as 'most of us/many of us/the majority of the group/only some of us/very few/none of us/etc.'

7   Allow the students to ask you any questions from the sheet they like.

NB   *Psychology questionnaires of the type required here can be found in* Challenge to Think, The Q-Book *and others.*

Impressing people

Level   Intermediate and above

Time   20-30 min.

Grammar structures   'Second' conditional, present simple

Preparation
Make copies of the box below so that every second student has a copy. Take Blu-tack to class.

In class

1   Pair the students and give A in each pair a copy of this box:

What do you What wouldn't you What don't you What would you	do to impress	a 9-year-old? your father? your husband/wife? a pensioner? a policeman? your mother? your boss? a school teacher? a 4-year-old? a boy/girl friend?

2   Make sure students understand the difference between the present simple questions and the conditional question; e.g., if you ask:

'What do you do to impress your boss?' you are assuming that the other person really tries to impress their boss.

If you ask:
'What would you do to impress your husband?' you are talking about an unreal or hypothetical situation.

3   Get A in each pair to put 5 questions from the above box to B and to write down the answers in full sentences. B then puts 5 questions to A and writes down the answers in full sentences.

4   Ask each student to hang their partner's answers on the wall. They circulate and read each other's sentences.

Near miss

Level   Intermediate and above

Time   15 min. in the first class and 30 min. in the second

Grammar structures   Past simple and 'third' conditional

In class

1   Tell the class a story about a near miss involving something that nearly happened to you or to someone dear to you. The story could be about something dreadful that you are relieved to have escaped or something wonderful that you regret having missed. Make sure that the event you choose still moves you and that this gets across to the students. End your story with a 'third' conditional sentence like this:

'If the lorry wheel'd been one centimetre nearer, the boy would've been crushed to death.'

'If I hadn't said that at the interview, I might well've landed the job.'

2   For homework, ask the students to prepare near-miss stories of their own, each ending with a sentence on the same pattern. Tell them not to write out their stories, but to prepare them orally, mumbling them to themselves.

In the next class

1   Find out how many students have near-miss stories with the required punchline sentence. Organise small groups with a couple of story-tellers in each. Warn the listeners that they will have to re-tell the stories they hear and that they should note down the punchlines they hear.

2   Ask the students to change groups and have the listeners tell the stories they have heard, with the punchlines. Ask the new listeners to keep a written note of the punchlines.

3   Have 4 or 5 students tell the whole class the best story they heard. After the telling, ask each of them to write up the punchline on the board.

Birthplaces

Level   Elementary and above

Time   15 min.

Grammar structures   Past simple of *to be born*

In class

1   Check out where people in the class were *brought up*. Ask a student to come out and draw a map covering the whole board showing the areas mentioned. Check that the map now shows all the areas in which group members were brought up.

2   Ask a third of the class to act as questioners and find out from the other two-thirds where they were *born*, asking 'Where were you born?' The questioners then write up the person's name and birthplace on the appropriate part of the map.

3   Ask the students to look at the map very carefully and to memorise the birthplaces. They must *not* take notes.

Rub the map and birthplaces out.

4   Get the students asking each other:

'Where was X born?'.

If no-one can remember, then X comes in with:

'I was born in...'

Rationale

We give a whole exercise to the above structure because it causes EFL students considerable difficulty, especially if German is their mother tongue.

♀ or ♂

Level   Intermediate and above

Time   30-40 min.

Grammar structures   'Second' and 'third' conditional

Preparation

Copy the completion sentences below enough times for each person to have one copy.

In class

1   Ask each student to imagine what life would be like were they a member of the other sex, and to individually complete the sentences you give out.

2   Ask the students to get out of their seats and to mill. When they are all up, ask each person to find a partner, if possible of the other sex, and explain their sentence completions to them. Get the students to re-pair 2 or 3 times.

Completion sentences

- If I was...
- If I belonged to the other sex...
- Had I been born (a)...
- Supposing I were (a)...
- My parents would've...
- If I wasn't the sex I am...
- Were I (a)...

ADD 10 more sentences of your own about what it would be like to belong to the other sex.

Acknowledgement

The idea of sexual role-reversal we learnt from Bernard Dufeu of Mainz University.

Gossip

Level Intermediate and above

Time 20-30 min.

Grammar structures Reported speech with past tense reporting verb, but without backshift (see grammar note in 'Labels', this section)

In class

1 Group the students in 4s. Ask one person in each 4 to come out of the room with you and to write their name on a slip of paper. They stay out of the room. You come back in, shuffle the slips of paper and give them out to the threesomes.

2 Ask A and B in each 3 to spend about 4 minutes telling each other everything they know about the person whose name they have been given. C in each group is to listen as hard as they can and take notes.

3 Call the people who are outside, back in. Assign each one to the group which has been talking about them. Each 'outsider' must find out from C what A and B have been saying about them. A and B must stay strictly silent.

   C is to report using this type of pattern:

   'A said you are ...' (i.e., not using backshift).

   When C's report is over, then A and B can object if they feel they have been wrongly reported. (D, of course, may also have something to say!)

4 Repeat the exercise, but with all the students in new roles.

Danger

We do not advise you to do this exercise unless you have a reasonably harmonious group, as it is evidently a frame within which people can be nasty to each other if they wish. Most people actually avoid this, as self-censorship is built into most of us.

Labels

Level   Intermediate and above

Time   30 min.

Grammar structures   Reported speech with past tense reporting verb but *without* using backshift.

'Backshift' is when you move the tenses back following a past tense reporting verb, e.g.:

Direct speech: 'I will see them at lunchtime.'
Indirect speech: She said she would see them at lunchtime.

Contrary to what many EFL books teach, it is quite possible to omit using backshift with a past tense reporting verb. In the example above it could be:

Indirect speech: She said she'll see them at lunchtime.

For a clear but partial explanation of when to backshift and when not to after a past tense reporting verb, refer to Unit 16 of *Well Said*, by Dixey and Rinvolucri, Pilgrims Publications.

Preparation

Get adhesive labels that can be safely stuck on clothing. Have 2 labels to each class member. Write an adjective descriptive of people on each label. Have many more positive than negative labels, e.g.:

thoughtful   odd
bright   gentle
dreamy   strong
old-fashioned   dominant
attractive

However have *some* negative, or possibly negative, labels, or the exercise gets slushy. You may decide to have some common adjectives on more than one label.

In class

1   Explain any of the adjectives that you feel will be unfamiliar to the group.

2   Put the labels up in front of the class in 3 or 4 strips so that the students can crowd round them and take a label. They are to stick a given adjective on someone else they feel it fits. As they stick the label on they *must tell* the person why they have chosen that label for them. The person must carefully register the explanation.

Nobody who has already got 3 labels stuck on them must be given any more.

Join in the exercise yourself!

3   Get the students back to their seats — these should be in a circle. Point to one of the labels stuck on you and say:

'X said *I'm* odd because I like pickled onions,' quoting the person who stuck it on you.

Draw attention to the use of a present tense after a past tense reporting verb.

4   Now ask the students to say what labels they have been given and to report what others said to them when they stuck the labels on.

Acknowledgement

We learnt this exercise from Carlos Maeztu.

Reactions

Level   Intermediate and above

Time   20-30 min.

Grammar structures   'Second' conditional

In class

1   Write the following sentences on the board:

You are stopped by the police for driving too fast.
You are told you need a serious operation.
Your dog bites a child.
You inherit a large sum of money.
You are made redundant.

2   Put the students in groups of 3.

3   Ask the students to write how they imagine they would react in any 3 of the situations on the board and how they imagine their 2 partners would react.

4   Allow about 15 min. for this writing stage.

5   Let the students read what their partners have written, ask questions about their partners' reactions and react to what their partners have written about them.

Variation

Tell each student to write down the names of 5 people, either friends or family members — they can include themselves in the list if they want to. Ask the students to imagine that each person on the list unexpectedly receives a large sum of money, say £50,000, maybe as an inheritance or from the lottery. Ask the students to write 3 sentences about how each of the 5 people on their list would or would not use the money.

Now pair the students and ask them to describe each of the 5 people on their list to their partner and then read out the sentences about them.

My names

Level   Elementary and above

Time   15-25 min.

Grammar structures   Present simple, past simple or 'used to' passive + by + when...

In class

1   Using the pattern:

I'm
I was   called... by... when...
I used to be

tell the students half a dozen names you are or have been known by, e.g.:

'I was called Mariolino by my father when he was feeling affectionate.'

2   Ask the students to write down as many sentences as they can using the above pattern, listing as many of their names and nicknames as they are willing to share with others.

3   Get the students up out of their seats and milling. They read their sentences to various partners and explain the contexts of the names.

Variation

This exercise frame can be used more than once to drill the present and past passive forms, by building in different verbs.

Ask the students to think back to before they were 10. Ask them to write as many sentences as they can using this pattern:

When I was... I was helped to... by...
e.g.: 'When I was 5½ I was helped to tie up my bootlaces by my teacher.'

Also ask them to write a few sentences on this pattern:

Nowadays I am helped to ... by...

Other verbs that lend themselves to this exercise include:

to be given, to be punished, to be blamed, to be rewarded, etc.

Blind advice-giving

Level   Lower intermediate and above

Time   20-40 min.

Grammar structures   Various ways of introducing suggestions

In class

1   Give the class this list of ways they can give advice:

Why don't you . . .
What if you + past
How about . . . + ing
If I were you, I'd . . .
Why not + infinitive

2   Ask the students to work in groups of 5 or 6. One person in each group is to think up a problem they have, the sort of problem they don't mind the others finding out about. Tell them not to tell the group they are in about the problem they have in mind. Tell the other students they are to give the student with the unknown problem advice. By listening to his/her reactions they will gradually find out what the problem is. They are *not* to ask any questions, just give advice.

3   Ask other people in the subgroups to come up with 'socialisable' problems of their own so the exercise can be repeated two or three times. (Some people may well not feel they have problems they want to share.)

Rationale

Some readers may think this is a barmy exercise. On closer reflection, though, it clearly mimics the reality of much advice giving. The advice-giver will often lavish her generous thoughts on the problem owner without any clear idea of how the problem looks, feels or sounds to the latter.

Acknowledgement

We learnt this exercise from watching a powerful interaction between Silvia Stefan and Gerry Kenny. Gerry proposed the exercise as it stands above. Silvia produced the stimulus.

My competence

Level   Elementary and above

Time   10 min.

Grammar structures   can/can't   must/needn't

In class

1   Say your name and something you can do and something you can't do, e.g.:

I'm Christine, I can play the piano, but I can't dance.

2   Each student introduces her/himself in the same way.

3   Some time later in the lesson ask the students in pairs to write down as many sentences as they can remember, e.g.:

Sonja can cook, but she can't speak Spanish, etc.

4   The sentences are circulated or put up round the walls to be read by everybody.

Variation

Depending on the structure being taught the statements can be changed, e.g.:

I'm . . . I must . . ., but I needn't . . .

Most structures will change in the third person e.g.:

I've got – she's got
I like – she likes

this must be taken into consideration when asking the students to write sentences from memory.

Family modals

Level   Lower intermediate and above

Time   20-40 min.

Grammar structures   should/shouldn't   Don't + infinitive
must/oughtn't to   Imperative
should've/ought to've . . .

Preparation

As homework ask students to collect oft-repeated parental utterances. If they are school students living at home ask them to bring a short list of negative parent sentences, things like 'John, you really should tidy your room'. If they are adults ask them to think back to their childhood, or to think of things they say to their own kids over and over again. If you have shortstay foreign students in an English speaking country you might ask them to come with a list of host-family utterances.

In class

1   Ask the students to write up three or four of their sentences on the board. In each case the student explains who used the sentence to whom, and the whole context. Some students will want to act out the utterances. (You will need to be ready to help with translation from the mother tongue.)

2   Where you take the class from this first stage is wide open. What you have on the board are sentences charged with emotion. Over to you.

Acknowledgement

We learnt this technique from Marcia Karp.

Parental control

Level   Intermediate

Time   10-15 min.

Grammar structures   Make/let somebody do something

In class

1   Get the students to sit in a large circle.

2   Start off by saying:

'At the age of eight my parents made me . . . , but they let me. . . .'
'At the age of fifteen my parents made me . . . , but they let me. . . .'

3   Each student in turn should make statements about themselves in this way.

4   When each student has recalled the 'Make' and 'Let' experiences ask them to write down what they can remember from what has been said in the group, e.g.:

'Sam's parents made him wash up, but let him stay out till 11 o'clock when he was 15.'

5   The student who writes the longest list, is the winner.

The boss

Level   Elementary and above

Time   20 min.

Grammar structures   'Second' conditional

In class

1   Tell the students to write down 5 words they would use to describe their boss. (With younger students, take headmaster/mistress.)

2   Ask the students to put their words on the blackboard and arrange them under the headings 'positive' and 'negative'.

3   Now write on the blackboard:

If I were my boss I'd....
If I had my boss's job I'd....
If I did my boss's job I'd....
If I were in my boss's position....

Ask the students to think of the positive and negative aspects of their bosses' job. Tell them to write 5 reasons why they would like to have the position of their boss (or headmaster) and 5 reasons for not wanting the job.

4   Encourage them to discuss the positive and negative aspects of being in a position of power.

This exercise works well if several students have the same 'boss'.

Animals

Level   Elementary and above

Time   30 min.

Grammar structures   'Second' conditional ('d/would)

Preparation

Make copies of the completion sentences below so that each student can be given a copy.

In class

1   Give each student a copy of these completion sentences:

If I was an animal	I'd like to be a/an... I think other people'd mostly see me as... My mother'd see me as... X, my brother/sister, would see me as... My father'd see me as...
If s/he was an animal	I'd see A, here in this group, as... I'd see B, here in this group, as... I'd see C, here in this group, as...

2   Ask the students to complete the sentences, working on their own.

3   Get the students up and milling so that they can explain their sentences to other people. Ask them to explain their sentences to one other person at a time. The reason for standing and moving round the room is that this allows people to choose the partners they want to work with. If you see students waiting too long for a partner, pair them off yourself.

Others do it for me

Level   Intermediate and above

Time   15-20 min.

Grammar structures   Passive infinitive

In class

1   Ask students round the class these questions:

Do you like to cook for yourself?   When? Why? Why not?
Do you like to be cooked for?   When? Why? Why not?
Do you like to read for yourself?   When? Why? Why not?
Do you like to be read to?   When? Why? Why not?
Do you like to give yourself things?   When? Why? Why not?
Do you like to be given things?   When? Why? Why not?

2   Pair the students. Ask them to work together and figure out actions they sometimes like to do and sometimes like others to do for them, e.g.:

I like to drive when...

I like to be driven when...

They should write their sentences down.

3   Get them up and milling. They tell each other their sentences and discuss them.

4   Finally bring the class together and see if there is any consensus of opinion on the occasions when they like other people to do things for them.

V

Other Grammar Areas

Old rubbish

Level   Beginner to post-beginner

Time   15-25 min.

Grammar structures   Personal pronouns + adjectives, personal adjectives

In class

1   Give your students the personal pronouns (mine, yours etc.) on the board and teach their use.

2   Tell the students to go outside the building and come back with three or four objects (perhaps rubbish) each (e.g. leaves, cigarette ends, twigs etc.)

3   Have the students, on their return, work in threes and make up sentences describing their objects:

Mine is old
Yours is dirty
Hers is plastic

They will need plenty of help with vocabulary, so you need to be as available as possible.

4   Having referred to their objects so far only by gesture and the use of pronouns teach the students the names of the objects they have collected.

5   Ask them to make further sentences, this time using personal adjectives:

My feather is light
Your can is red

Rationale

Movement is vital in language learning. For some people a brief escape from the classroom is a relief. People choose the objects they bring back and therefore feel some association with them.

Acknowledgement

We learnt the rubbish collecting idea from Tessa Woodward, author of Loop Input. *She gets people to compare their rubbish: 'My pebble is rounder than yours'.*

114

Describing people

Level   Upper intermediate to advanced

Time   30–45 min.

Grammar structures   Compound qualitative adjectives for describing people. This list is based on the one in the Collins *Cobuild English Grammar*. It therefore reflects the reality of the language.

Preparation

Copy the list below so you have one copy for each pair of students.

In class

1   Give this list of compound adjectives to each pair of students:

absent-minded	nice-looking	swollen-headed
accident-prone	off-putting	tender-hearted
big-headed	old-fashioned	thick-skinned
cold-blooded	open-minded	tongue-tied
easy-going	second-class	two-faced
good-looking	second-rate	warm-hearted
good-tempered	short-sighted	well-balanced
hard up	short-tempered	well-behaved
kind-hearted	slow-witted	well-dressed
laid-back	smooth-talking	well-known
light-hearted	soft-hearted	well-off
long-suffering	starry-eyed	worldly-wise
low-paid	strong-minded	wrong-headed
muddle-headed	stuck-up	
narrow-minded	sun-tanned	

If the level is right they will know many of them already. Ask them to work through the rest with their partner, with a dictionary or with your help, so that all are known.

2   The students now work separately. Ask each person to draw a sociogram with themselves at the centre. Mine might look like this:

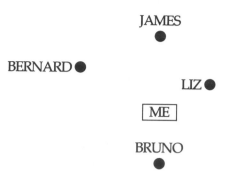

Do a sociogram of your own on the board. Explain to the students what the relationship of the other people is to you. So, in my diagram, Bruno is my small son, James is my boss etc. Tell the students to include 5 to 7 people in their sociograms.

3   Ask them to look through the adjective list and pick half-a-dozen adjectives that accurately describe their closest person. They do the same with each of the other people on their sociogram.

4   They work with new partners (of their choice) and explain their sociograms and adjectives. Encourage them to fill out the picture of the people they are thinking about.

Rationale

With the appearance of the *Cobuild Grammar*, based on the massive Birmingham University language corpus, we can now confidently give students restricted word category lists, like the one above, in the secure knowledge that these are the most frequent and therefore mose useful exponents within their word class.

You remind me of

Level   Elementary to intermediate

Time   15-30 min.

Grammar structures   To remind someone of/to remember to make someone think of . . . , different from/different to, comparatives

Preparation

Get hold of a soft ball or make one from crumpled newspaper.

In class

1   Remind the class of the comparative structures. Check that they know *different from/to*. Give them these structures on the board:

You remind me of . . .
You make me think of
When I see/hear you, I remember . . .

2   If possible seat the students in a circle. Look round the group yourself and see if there is anybody in this group that reminds you of someone else you know (it could be their hair, their eyes, their walk . . .). If there *is* someone then throw them the ball and say:

'You remind me of X because . . .'

Having given the similarities, then add:

'You are different from X because . . .'

You may find that you do not have a projection to share. Don't 'invent' one. It will ring hollow. If you have nothing to say place the ball in the centre of the group, explain the exercise to the students and ask whichever of them has a projection to share to take the ball and throw it to the relevant person. In a group of 20 to 40 people there are always plenty of projections around, whether this is the first week of the course or some way into it.

Rationale

The exercise is linguistically useful as a powerful, meaningful language drill. It is also useful group-dynamically as the sort of projections described above exist in each and every group and get in the way of the students meeting each other properly.

The exercise, though, can cause pain. Students who are not singled out by others sometimes feel bad about it. Some students are unhappy if they trigger an association with a nasty person in another's mind.

Acknowledgement

We learnt this activity from the psychodramatist Barbara Tregear.

Describing contraries

Level   Intermediate and above

Time   30 min.

Grammar structures   Vocabulary enrichment (adjectives)

Preparation
Bring in about 15 interesting pictures taken from magazines and newspapers.

In class
1   Ask the students to list adjectives individually to describe a good friend, an enemy, a place where they feel happy, and a place where they feel uncomfortable.

2   Go round helping with words they do not know. Ideally the students should have four lists of 5 or 6 words.

3   In groups of about 4 let them explain why they chose the adjectives they did and get them to collect all the adjectives that have been suggested by their group.

4   Ask them to write the adjectives on single slips of paper.

5   Give each group 3 or 4 pictures and tell them to lay the slips of paper on that picture which they think is most appropriate.

6   The pictures are left spread out on the tables and all the students circulate to have a look at the pictures and adjectives of the other groups and if necessry ask for reasons or explanation for their choice.

How often?

Level   Elementary and above

Time   20-30 min.

Grammar structures   Adverbs of frequency + present simple

In class

1   Divide your class up into groups of 6-8. Have the students put their names on slips of paper which they then fold over. One person in each group collects in the slips and shuffles them. Each person in the group takes a slip, but no-one must take their own. If they do, get them to exchange it for another slip.

2   Write up on the board:

```
I always .....
I         .....
I         .....
I         .....
I         .....
I         .....
I never   .....
```

Elicit from the students the adverbs and adverbial phrases of frequency between *always* and *never*. The list might include *often/sometimes/occasionally/hardly ever* etc.

3   Now tell the students they are to become the person whose name they have. Make sure that the idea of identity exchange is clear by asking students:

'You used to be called Juan, who are you now?' In their new identity they are to write one first-person sentence for each adverb of frequency which is up on the board. In doing this, they will be describing habits they know or suppose the other person to have. As they write, go round behind helping them.

4   Within the groups, ask student A to say who they were writing as. Ask them to read the sentences one by one. Student B, the person written about, has a right of reply after each sentence. If B agrees then the reply is simply *yes*; if B disagrees then they correct student A within the structure:

A (speaking as B) : 'I always go to church on Sundays.'
B (objecting)   : 'No, I *never* go to church on Sundays.'

5   Have each of the students in the sub-groups read out their projections and get them corrected by their 'victim'. The work in the sub-groups is to go on simultaneously.

How I think, how you think

Level   Elementary and above

Time   20-30 min.

Grammar structures   Adjectives + present simple

In class

1   Ask each student to write 5 adjectives to describe him/herself and then 5 adjectives s/he thinks the group would use to describe him or her.

2   Collect the papers and read the first 5 adjectives from one of the papers.

3   Get the group to guess who is describing him/herself.

4   When the owner has been identified, return the paper to them and ask them to read the words they wrote that they think the group would have chosen to describe them.

5   Let the group comment on this second list of adjectives.

6   Go through 4 or 5 papers in this way and then put the remainder of papers on the walls for students to read and discuss or comment on as they wish.

Eat, smile, dance!

Level   Elementary and above

Time   20 min.

Grammar structures   Adverb building + present simple interrogative

In class

1   Write up on the board: EAT
                                        SMILE
                                        DANCE

   Ask the students if they always eat, smile and dance in the same way.
   Does it depend on who they are with...?

2   Get the students to write between 5 and 10 questions (depending on the size of
   the class), each addressed to named people in the group asking how they
   smile, eat or dance in particular situations, e.g.:

   'Mark, how do you smile at your boss?'
   'Maria, how do you eat when your grandfather comes to lunch?'

   Go round and help the students during this writing phase.

3   The students now fire their questions at each other across the room, with you
   at the board building up a list of the adverbs used in the replies. The replies
   need only be adverbs or adverbial phrases, but if you want to practise word
   order, encourage complete sentences. In some cases you will have to help
   supply a particular adverb a student is groping for.

4   Ask a student to come out and give orders to the others using the 3 verbs and
   the adverbs from the board, e.g.:

   'Juana, eat greedily!'
   'Akiro, smile sweetly!'

Acknowledgement

*This exercise was born in a British Council workshop in Paris in January 1978, and Michael Swan
was probably the main originator.*

Objects in a bag

Level   Beginners to elementary

Time   20 min.

Grammar structures   Possessive pronouns and adjectives

Preparation

Bring a large bag to class.

In class

1   Ask all the students to shut their eyes. With eyes shut, ask them to choose 2 objects from their handbags, pockets or wallets and to put these into your bag as you come round. They can now open their eyes. (With young children, check for cheating.)

2   Ask one student to come and stand behind the class, with their back to the class. Let them feel inside your bag and choose an object, not one of their own, and take it out without the class seeing what it is. Still with their back to the group, they describe the object taken: size, colour, shape, feel, etc.

Members of the class now hypothesise whose it is. They are not allowed to mention anyone by name: they say,

'It's his/hers because...' (they point).

Finally the owner says 'It's mine' and gets the property back.

3   The process is repeated with further students.

4   Make sure that at the end of the exercise everybody gets their things back safely.

Describing others

Level   Intermediate and above

Time   30–40 min.

Vocabulary enrichment   Descriptive adjectives

In class

1   Give examples of 3 women you know well — write their names on the board. Next to each name write down 5 adjectives that you feel describe the person. Focus on adjectives that describe personality.

2   Now ask each student to establish a list of:

   3 girls/women they know well
   3 boys/men they know well
   3 people from within the class group.

   Next to each name, the student now writes 5 adjectives that describe the person. While this is going on, you should circulate and help people with words they can't find in English. Encourage use of dictionaries and students helping each other.

3   Group the students in 3s. Ask them to explain who the people they have written down are, expand the 5 adjectives into fuller descriptions, and give an idea of what the people look like.

Danger

If you are not a native speaker of English the students may well want adjectives you are not sure of in English. To get over this problem and to learn alongside your students, make sure you bring a large bilingual dictionary to class.

We'll put you in an ad

Level   Intermediate and above

Time   45 min.

Vocabulary enrichment   Adjectives

Preparation

Cut out 30 to 50 adjectives from magazine and newspaper adverts. Mix adjectives you think the students will know with ones that will be new to them. Make an adjective collage and photocopy it so you can give out one collage to each pair of students. Bring in Blu-tack.

In class

1   Ask the class to pair off and give each pair the collage. Ask them to work through the adjectives making sure they understand all of them. Tell them to ask each other, to use dictionaries and to ask you.

2   Now ask the students to decide what sort of ad each adjective came from.

3   Ask the pairs to choose someone in the group who they want to include in an ad for some commodity, service or political idea. They then choose adjectives to fit, and write the text of the ad round a pin-person drawing of the person they've chosen. Go round helping with finding new adjectives they may need.

4   Have them hang their adverts on the walls. People go round and read each other's, maybe looking for themselves.

Variation

Give out English language magazines and newspapers and have the students make adjective collages for themselves. This could lead into an exchange of collages within the group and a re-run of the exercise above. Alternatively you take in their collages and use them for work with another class.

The same sort of work can be done with other lexical categories, e.g. adverbs, verbs, abstract nouns etc...

The others compared to me

Level   Elementary and above

Time   15-25 min.

Grammar structures   Comparatives

In class

1   Have the students sit in circles of 7 or 8. Tell them to each write one sentence comparing each other person in the group to them, e.g.:

'Hilda is a little more intelligent than me.'
'I am probably older than George.'

If there are 7 other people in the group each student in that group will need to write 7 sentences. Make it clear that they must not compare two classmates; don't accept a sentence like:

'Hilda is fatter than George.'

The writers themselves must be part of each comparative sentence.

2   In each group, get the students to read out all their sentences about person A, and then all their sentences about person B, etc...

Variation

This exercise frame can well be used to work on the superlative. In this case each student has to write a superlative sentence about each other student in the group, e.g.:

'Hilda is the most hard-working student in the group.'
'George is the youngest of us,' etc...

Acknowledgement

We learnt this exercise from Pfeiffer & Jones.

Hands

Level   Intermediate

Time   30-40 min.

Grammar structures   Comparatives and superlatives

In class

1   Ask a student who is good at drawing to come out and draw you 2 large
    hands on the board (3 times life size). Ask him or her to draw one hand palm
    up and the other palm down.

    Elicit from the group the vocabulary needed to describe a hand. You should
    end up with a list like this:

wrist	ring finger	vein
palm	little finger	skin
thumb	nail	heart line
forefinger	knuckle	head line
middle finger	line	life line

    Write the *new* words on the 2 hands on the board.

2   Pair the students and ask them to compare their hands with their partner's
    from as many aspects as possible, using structures like:

    a bit less... than...
    rather more... than...
    quite a lot ...er than...
    not nearly as... as...

3   Have the students stand in a circle. Designate one student to go round looking
    for the biggest hand in the group. When they find it, they say:

    'X has the biggest hand in the group.'

    Designate successive students to find:

the cleanest hand	the most interesting hand
the broadest hand	the strongest heart line
the dirtiest hand	the longest fingers
the warmest hand	the stubbiest thumb
the youngest hand	the longest nails
the coldest hand	the longest life line
the driest hand	the shortest fingers

How others see me

Level   Elementary and above

Time   20 min.

Vocabulary enrichment   Adjectives

In class

1   Write the following questions on the blackboard:

How would your best friend describe you?

How would your parents describe you?

How would your children describe you?

How would your class-mate/colleague describe you?

How would your boyfriend/girlfriend/husband/wife describe you?

2   Tell the students to choose one of these questions and to think of 5 adjectives they could give as an answer. Each student should write his 5 words on a large piece of paper.

3   Hang the papers around the room and let the students speculate on 'who was describing who', e.g. one student commenting on 'moody, difficult, stubborn, intelligent, generous' may say, 'I think that is Juan's parents describing Juan.'

Students can then confirm or deny these statements. At this stage, also encourage students to ask questions about any adjectives they are unfamiliar with.

Do we all agree?

Level   Elementary and above

Time   20 min.

Grammar structures   We all, none of us, etc...

In class

1   Write up on the board:

We all	think money makes people happy.
...	like the colour blue.
...	feel sex before marriage is wrong.
...	...
...	...
...	...
None of us	...

Elicit from the class the quantifiers missing between *we all* and *none of us*. Write them in as the students give them to you, supplying any they can't come up with.

The list might include: most of us
many of us
some of us
a few of us
hardly any of us

Ask the students to make suggestions about filling the 4 empty lines on the right of the board with controversial statements. Pick their 4 best suggestions.

2   Ask the students to work on their own and write down 6 sentences in which they hazard a guess about the whole class's attitude to the propositions on the right. One student might write:

'Most of us like the colour blue.'

3 Invite several students to read out their sentences about money.
Now ask the group to vote on the propositions:

'Money makes people happy.'

In this way the students can check if their impression of the group's thinking
was correct or not. On the blackboard, join the halves of the sentences on the
right with the appropriate expressions on the left.

Treat the other 5 statements in the same way.

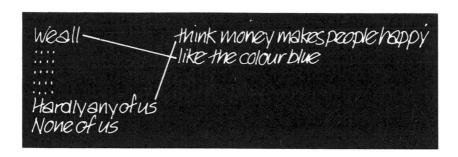

Variation

You can use this exercise shape for revising vocabulary:

We all . . .   know   ⎧ the 10 to 15
None of us   knows   ⎩ words to be revised

Ban the use of dictionaries and write up the lexis to be revised to the right. Ask the
students to work in pairs guessing which words the group knows and which it does
not.

Instead of voting, as in step 3 above, you get people to volunteer the meaning of the
word. You confirm or correct. The process of working with the words fixes them
firmly in the students' heads.

How many have you got?

Level   Beginners to elementary

Time   15 min.

Grammar structures   How much/how many; a few/a little/ a lot of/lots
of etc...

In class

1   Ask a student to come out in front of the group and repeatedly ask you the
same question: 'How many have you got?' Ask the student to occasionally
change the question to: 'How much have you got?' Each time the student asks
you these 'empty' questions you give 'full' answers, e.g.:

Student: How much have you got?
You: I've got plenty of time.
Student: How many have you got?
You: I've got about 200 books.
Student: How many have you got?
You   I've got 2 children, etc...

After about 10-15 answers, change roles with the student and put the same
questions repeatedly to him/her.

2   Now pair the students. Ask them to repeat the exercise as above. Tell them it
is best to talk about real things, not just make up items they don't have. Tell
them to try and go on as long as they can bring themselves to, inventing new
answers to the same questions. The answers tend to get more interesting the
longer the answerer is able to carry on.

Rationale

The student asking the question seems to be simply doing a boring, repetitive drill.
This is not true, though, as the intonation of the question often changes in
response to the way the last answer came out.

The answerer is exploring different ways of answering the same question and has a
fascinating, though sometimes anxiety-provoking, task. It is the richness of their
answers that makes the exercise interesting for the question-asker.

Many teachers, when they first come across this kind of insistence exercise, want to allow the questioner to vary the questions. If you do this you much reduce the answerer's task and reduce the exercise to quasi-naturalistic dialogue of great banality. The insistence exercise purposely breaks the normal rules of discourse in order to provide an idea-and-grammar-structure-exploring frame.

Acknowledgement

We learnt the idea of 'insistence exercises' from Richard Baudins. Dierk Andresen has also helped the development of this family of exercises.

Us two

Level   Elementary and above

Time   15-25 min.

Grammar structures   Both of us, one of us, neither of us

In class

1   Write up on the board:

	like(s) music.
	is/are (a) leader(s).
	is/are angry.
Both of us	feel(s) shy.
One of us	prefer(s) rice to...
Neither of us	is/are afraid of growing old.
	...
	...
	...

2   Pair the students. Ask them to copy the sentences down and invent 3 more propositions. Ask them to do this in writing without talking to one another.

3   Ask each student, again without talking to their partner, to decide which quantifier phrase is correct for the 2 of them in the 9 contexts now given.

4   Pair the pairs. In 4s, the students read out the sentences they think are right and see if this is the case, by checking with their partners.

Places I am in

Level Elementary to intermediate

Time 30-40 min.

Grammar structures Spatial prepositions

Preparation

Copy the completion sentences opposite so that each student can have a copy.

In class

1 Give each student a copy of the sentences and ask them to complete them using spatial prepositions, without talking to their neighbours.

2 Put the students in 3s and ask them to read out their completed sentences to their partners, taking time to explain and give any background information that may be needed.

'Places I am in' completion sentences

(i)   When I go into an empty restaurant, I usually sit _____

_____

(ii) In a cinema I like to sit _____

because _____

(iii) On a bus I tend to sit_____

(iv) On a train I prefer to find a seat_____

(v)   When I am with my family at mealtimes I sit_____

my _____

(vi) My favourite place in the living room is _____

(vii) When I look out of my bedroom window I see _____

and _____

(viii) I prefer to sleep with my head towards _____

(ix) It takes me _____

to get_____my home _____ my

school/workplace.

(x)   When I first went to primary school, I sat _____

the_____ row.

(xi) When I first went to secondary school I sat _____

the maths teacher.

(xii) When I was a small child my favourite place in the living room was _____

_____

Where do you live?

Level   Beginner to elementary

Time   15 min.

Grammar structures   Spatial prepositions and present simple interrogative and declarative

In class

1   Ask a student to come out in front of the group and repeatedly ask you the same question: 'Where do you live?' You have to give as many different answers as you can, e.g.:

Student: Where do you live?
You: Wassermann St., No. 7.

Student: Where do you live?
You: Well, I live in a small town.

Student: Where do you live?
You: In a modern house with three bedrooms.

Student: Where do you live?
You: In a street where nobody talks to their neighbours.

Reverse the process and put the same question repeatedly to the student. Each person should produce 20 or 30 different answers to the same question.

2   Pair the students. Ask them to repeat the exercise as above, with one person asking, 'Where do you live?' over and over again and with the other trying to answer in as many different ways as possible.

Go round listening to the things going wrong with their prepositions and supplying vocabulary they need.

After the pair work, help them with the prepositions that they got wrong.

Am I the same as the picture?

Level   Elementary and above

Time   15-20 min.

Grammar structures   So do you, neither have I, etc.

Preparation

Choose a picture large enough for the whole group to see. The picture should feature 2 or 3 people doing something eye-catching, e.g., fighting, kissing etc.

In class

1   Ask the students to each write *simple* comments about the actions or appearance of the people in the picture, e.g.:

The man's got a beard.
She doesn't look happy.
She's hitting him.
He isn't rich.

2   Write up these patterns on the board:

So've		So've		So's	
So'm		So're		Neither's	she
Neither've		Neither've		So does	he
Neither'm	I	Neither're	you	Neither does	
So do		So do			
Neither do		Neither do			

3   Ask a student to read out a comment on the picture. Other students relate the comment to members of the group, e.g.:

A: (referring to the picture) 'The man's got a beard.'
B: 'So's Mike!' (another student in the group)
C: 'So've I!'

If Mike doesn't have a beard, he should object.

4   Repeat step 3 until the group begins to switch off — keep the pace fast.

From your window

Level   Elementary and above

Time   30-40 min. in class 1
         10-15 min. in class 2

Grammar structures   The language of landscape description: e.g. in the foreground, behind, above, to the left of etc.

Preparation

Bring 2 pairs of binoculars to class.

To do this exercise successfully you need to be in a classroom with an extensive view. It won't work if your classroom window faces a blank wall across the street.

In class

1   Give the binoculars to a couple of students. Ask them and the rest of the group to spend a measured 90 seconds looking intently at the land- or city- or sea-scape beyond the window.

2   Ask the students to remain standing but with their backs to the window. They pair off and tell each other what they have seen. Get the binocular students to work together.

3   Bring the binocular pair to the front. The group questions them about what they have seen. You help with language and write up necessary phrases on the board.

4   Take the class back to the window and give different students a chance to practice some of the new language.

5   As homework ask them to choose one window in their flat or house and write a detailed description of the view seen from it.

6   *In the next class*, they hand in their descriptions and then pair off and give oral descriptions to their partner. You give back the written descriptions and the pairs check whether there were differences between the oral and the written texts.

Variation

John Morgan was teaching in a room in Athens with a great block of flats opposite. These were occupied by student squatters and the wall was covered with graffiti. John asked the group to choose empty bits of wall and to write or draw what they would like to see there – they drew on their own large pieces of paper! Teachers are often inspired to new exercises by what lies beyond the window.

Acknowledgement

I learnt to link visualisation with memory while working with John Morgan on Once Upon a Time, *Cl.iP, 1984.*

Contradiction

Level   Elementary

Time   15-20 min.

Grammar structures

To be + age	Of course not
to weigh . . .	I certainly { am not / don't . . .
to be . . . tall	
to take size . . . shoes	Rubbish!

In class

1   Ask each student to write 10 sentences in the second person about other students in the group and their brothers and sisters. They are to write about height, weight, age and shoe size. Tell them to estimate all this *wrong*:

'Helmut, you are 2 metres tall' (Helmut being on the short side).

2   Get them to memorise their sentences by saying them to themselves several times, quietly.

3   Ask them to get up and move around and say their sentences to the relevant people who contradict them with their real height, age etc. This is a fast-paced exercise.

NB   *The exercise is particularly suitable for pre- and early teenage students.*

Variation

The contradiction frame can be applied to many structures. People can write about the experience of others (present perfect) but getting it all wrong: 'you've had 6 children, haven't you' and this said to someone with 3.

Acknowledgement

We learnt the contradiction idea from Michele Maldonado, who works in français langue étrangère.

Sentence destruction

Level   Elementary and above

Time   15-25 min.

Grammar structures   The thing I like about . . . is . . .
What I like about . . . is . . .
The best thing about . . . is . . .

In class

1   Seat the class in circles of 8 to 10. If you have fixed benches you can still organise the students into groupings of 8 to 10.

2   Ask each person to think of something reasonably important that they really like. Each student takes a sheet of paper and writes a sentence about this important thing/situation/person. . . .

3   Each student passes their paper to the person on their right. The person receiving the sentence has to change its meaning as radically as possible by taking out 2 words anywhere in the sentence and by adding 2 words anywhere in the sentence. Suppose A receives this sentence:

'The thing I like about horse riding is being in harmony with the animal.' She might take out *like* and *harmony* and replace them with *hate* and *competition*: 'The thing I hate about horse riding is being in competition with the animal.' Another student might take out *in harmony* and add in *think you*: 'The thing I think you like about horse riding is being with the animal.'

Once the student has written down his/her radically changed sentence, he/she folds the top sentence over so it is hidden. He/she then passes the paper to the person on his/her right, who again modifies it, and so on round.

4   When the paper has gone round the group of 8 to 10 people it gets back to the original writer of the sentence. They now unfold the paper and see the transformations their sentence has been through.

NB   *Each transformation must leave a grammatical and meaningful sentence.*

Variation

The technique can be used to get students to explore a composition topic. They do this exercise with a theme sentence. A good way of generating a lot of ideas quickly.

Acknowledgement

The idea of this exercise came from seeing the work of an art therapist. Trish asked each person to make a mark they liked on the paper before them. They then passed the paper to their right. Their neighbour was asked to 'destroy' what they had drawn.

Things people do to you

Level   Intermediate and above

Time   50-60 min.

Grammar structures   Past tense verb + animate object + to + infinitive

In class

1   Put this verb list up on the board:

advised	forbade	warned
compelled	persuaded	encouraged
begged	taught	tempted

Make sure that the students understand what each word means.

2   Ask the group:

Can you remember a person who once advised you to do or not to do something?
Can you remember a person who tempted you to do something? etc.

Ask each student to write one sentence for each of the verbs above, drawing on their real experience, like this:

Last year X warned me not to...
In 1981 Y persuaded me to...

Stress that the exercise will be boring if they write fictitious sentences. Also make it clear that if they can't find a real experience for a particular verb they can omit to write a sentence.

3   Pair the students. They read their sentences to each other and fill out the background to each sentence.

4   Invite 10 or so students to choose their partner's most interesting sentence and write it on the board. Each of them tells the group of the circumstances round the partner's sentence.

5   Now ask the whole group if they prefer being begged or persuaded to do something, being compelled or warned etc...

6   Ask each student to write the 9 verbs out in order of preference with good at the top and bad at the bottom, depending on how much they like being the *objects* of these verbs.

7   Pair the students and ask them to explain their ranking to a partner.

I remember

Level   Intermediate

Time   In the first class 15-20 min. and 20 min. in the second

Grammar structures   remember, forget to + infinitive;
remember, forget + ... ing

In class

1   Tie a knot in your hankerchief or tell the students how you normally remember things; ask the students how they remember things — discuss cultural and personal ways.

2   Ask each student to write 7 sentences about things they and members of their family are scared of forgetting/must remember, e.g.

I must remember to...
Paul mustn't forget to...
My father finds it hard to remember to...

3   Ask them to work with a partner and explain the background to the sentences they have written.

In the next class

1   Tell the students about a dream of yours, an accident or an illness, starting most of your sentences with:

I remember... ing...

2   Put these sentence starters up on the board:

I think I remember ... ing
I'll never forget ... ing
I remember ...ing my...
I don't clearly remember ...ing

Ask the students to think back to a dream, accident or illness of theirs and write half a dozen 'remember' and 'forget' sentences.

3   Get the students to work in 3s and tell their stories to their partners.

Lavatories, trains and stations

Level   Lower intermediate and above

Time   30-40 min.

Grammar structures   *Do* + infinitive   *Do not* + infinitive

In class

1   Briefly revise the negative imperative and present Do + infinitive as in:
     'Please *do* come and see us when you are next here.'
     '*Do* sit down'.

2   Dictate these words to the group:

not	station	lavatory
use	in	is
when	train	do

Ask them to work in pairs and make three meaningful sentences with the nine words above + *the* used once, twice or three times in each of the sentences. Tell them they must use all 9 words plus between 1 and 3 *thes*.

3   Ask them to get up and move about, finding out what sentences other people have found.

4   Tell the students to make 3 columns on a sheet in front of them. They head the columns this way:

MEANINGFUL   IFFY   MEANINGLESS

Ask them to take down the following sentences you will dictate and to write them down in the column they think appropriate:

- Do not use when the lavatory train is in the station.
- Do not train when the station lavatory is in use.
- Do the lavatory when the train, not the station, is in use.
- Do not use the lavatory when the train is in the station.
- Do not use the station when the lavatory is in the train.
- Do use the lavatory when the train is not in the station.
- Do use the lavatory, . . . not when the train is in the station.
- Use the lavatory, not the train, when 'Do' is in the station.
- Do use the station lavatory when the train is not in.

5   Ask the students to work in pairs to compare their semantic decisions.

6   As homework ask the students to come next time with any stories they have about trains, lavatories or stations.

Acknowledgement

There is a similar semantic exercise in Dictation, *Davis, CUP.*

Last year's feelings

Level   Intermediate and above

Time   30 min.

Grammar structures   Verb + gerund

In class

1   Ask the students to write down one thing that happened to them last year in each of the following months:

January   April   July   October

Ask them to tell their neighbour about the events.

2   Put this verb list on the board:

avoided	postponed	resisted
enjoyed	loathed	denied
finished		

Make sure the students understand what each word means.

3   Ask the students to try and remember things they avoided doing last year and things they postponed doing last year, etc... Tell them to write one sentence for each verb, like this:

In July I ...ed ... +ing ...

Ask them to write about things that really happened, or the exercise will be boring. Make clear that if they can't find an experience for a verb they should not write a false sentence for that verb.

4   Pair the students. They explain the background of their sentences to their partners.

Different roles

Level   Elementary and above

Time   20-30 min.

Grammar structures   Want + pronoun + infinitive

In class

1   Write the following questions on the board:

Who does/did your best friend want you to be?

Who does/did your father want you to be?

Who does/did your girlfriend/boyfriend/husband/wife want you to be?

Who does/did your mother want you to be?

Who does/did your brother/sister/twin want you to be?

Who does/did your teacher want you to be?

Who does/did your subordinate want you to be?

Who does/did your boss want you to be?

Who does/did your conscience want you to be?

2   Tell the students to answer at least 4 of the questions in writing — give them the patterns:

X	wants doesn't want didn't want wanted	me to

3   Get the students in 3s or 4s. Ask each person to explain their different roles to the others. Join in the activity yourself and explain your own different roles in life.

Likes and dislikes

Level   Elementary

Time   20 min.

Grammar structures   Like/dislike + personal pronoun + gerund

In class

1   Draw 5 concentric circles on the board. Mark yourself at the centre and dot in 5 people who know you well; closest to the centre should be those people closest to you emotionally.

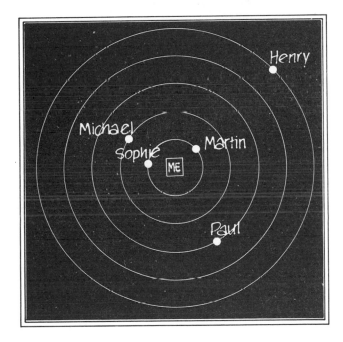

2   Ask the students to do the same, marking in 5 people who know them well, in order of closeness.

3   Now ask each student to write a sentence about what each person in their diagram loves or likes them doing and one sentence about what each person in the diagram dislikes or hates them doing, e.g., from the diagram above:

Martin likes me buying him chocolate.
Martin hates me trying to get him to go to bed early.

4   Group the students in 4s. Ask them to show each other their diagrams, read each other their sentences and explain the background.

What I borrowed, what I lent

Level   Elementary and above

Time   20 min.

Grammar structures   Past simple, lend, borrow

In class

1   Make sure the students understand the difference between 'to lend' and 'to borrow'.

2   Ask each student to think of the most important thing they have ever borrowed from somebody or the most important thing they have ever lent to somebody.

3   Have the students work in groups of 6. Invite individual students to share their experiences with the rest of the group, getting them to explain why they lent/borrowed something and how they felt on these occasions.

N.B. For some students the difference between 'to lend' and 'to borrow' presents problems at even the intermediate level.

VI
Free Work

Introduction

Most of this book deals with exercises that get students practising specific structures or groups of structures. This last section aims at free production, without any specified structural aim.

Part of a programme, whatever the level or age of the students, should consist of activities where the sole object is self-expression with whatever language resources the students possess or half-possess. Many teachers find this part of the programme hard to organise, as traditional conversation or discussion classes often end up as sessions in which the teacher questions more able members of the group about their opinions, with the less able students half-listening to what is going on.

What we propose in this section is a variety of exercise frames that allow the students to produce freely and which, as much as possible, involves everybody in the room. The teacher is not forced to take the role of central focal point, but has time to act as a resource person, supplying language when and where it is needed. To many colleagues this may feel a welcome change of role from the one they got pushed into in the traditional 'discussion class'.

How many threes in a five?

Level   Post-beginner and above

Time   10-20 min.

In class

1   Ask the students to work in groups of 3. Ask them to find out, anyway they like, how many different combinations of 3 they can find from the fingers of one hand, e.g.:

Combination A   Combination B

(Here the thumb is thought of as a finger)

Don't interfere in the triads' progress. Only give linguistic help, if you are asked. Enjoy yourself observing the group.

2   Ask each group for their answer. Accept answers like 8, 10, 12 and 20 non-judgementally. Tell them you are not interested in the right answer. Ask each group to tell you the story of their system, of how they got to their particular solution. Show your interest in the process.

Rationale

People do not expect to have to do mathematical thinking in a language class. They therefore meet each other on different ground from where they expected to be and show different sides of themselves.

We would not use this as an ice-breaker with a mathematically-able group as they tend to go straight for a pre-set formula and so reveal little human about themselves, beyond routine efficiency.

Acknowledgement

We learnt this exercise from Dick Tahta, A Silent Way, Gattegno-trained mathematics teacher.
The answer is . . . oh, we've forgotten!

Distant places

Level   Intermediate

Time   20 min.

Preparation

Bring in 6 large sheets of paper with the name of a country or place on each one, e.g. Scotland, Palestine, Hong Kong, Rumania, Colombia, Japan.

In class

1   Pin the papers on the walls and ask the students to walk round and write on anything they know about the countries.

2   Encourage the students to fill the papers with as many statements as possible.

3   After some time ask the students to stop writing, and read out what has been written.

4   Tell them to group themselves around a paper of their choice and to mark the sentences (highlighters are good for this) according to whether the statements are fact or opinion. This decision-making usually involves a good deal of discussion.

5   Put the papers back on the wall and let all the students read and comment on the fact or opinion decisions.

Variation

This exercise also works well with famous people or students from the class.

Landscape your mood

Level   Elementary and above

Time   20 min., or 45 including vocabulary follow-up

In class

1   Make sure that the students are familiar with the words

   seascape   landscape   cityscape

2   In a very gentle, non-aggressive way, ask various students what sort of mood they are in. One or two-word replies are fine.

3   Ask the students to shut their eyes and see their mood of the moment as a landscape. Shut your own eyes and concentrate to enchance the feeling in the group.

4   Ask half a dozen students to describe to the whole group the landscapes they saw. Help them with words they can't find and jot down useful and newish words on the board as they are used.

5   You may end up with a board covered with new words. Since the words will not stick in the students' minds unless they do something with them, use one of the many vocabulary revision techniques suggested in Morgan & Rinvolucri (1984).

Example

Here are some of the landscapes brought to mind by the exercise in one elementary class of German-speaking Swiss late teenagers and young adults:

- Swans on a lake covered in water lilies with reeds all round the edge.
- A field of red, red, poppies — a blaze of colour.
- The African bush, long thin grass, antelopes grazing.
- Two people side by side in a small English town, punts on the river, the sun setting.

Acknowledgement

We learnt this technique from Leveton (1977).

Statements about me

Level   Elementary and above

Time   40 min.

In class

1   Ask the students to write 20 statements about themselves and to make some of them *true*, some of them *half true* and some of them *false*. Make sure the students work on their own, without communicating. Go round helping them with words they need and checking on what they are writing.

2   Put the students in groups of 3 or 4. In each group Student A reads the first statement about him/herself and the others try to decide if it is true, half true or false. Finally A tells them. B then reads his/her first statement, etc...

Note of a parallel development

Andrew Wright, one of the authors of Games for Language Learning, CUP, 1979, *has recently told us of one of his techniques for making traditional essay-writing less boring. The teacher sets the subject for the essay and asks each student to include in it 5 false statements. When the class next meets, the students pair off and read each other their essays — the listener's task is to pick out the 5 false statements.*

Family trees

Level   Elementary and above

Time   30 min.

In class

1   Go over vocabulary connected with family relationships, e.g. sister-in-law, cousin (used for both sexes), parents, etc.

2   Put the students into groups of 6-8. (This exercise doesn't work well in a class of less than 12.) You should have a minimum of 2 groups and always an *even number* of groups.

3   Each group chooses a leader who draws and explains their family tree to the rest of their group. They allocate a member of their family to each person in the group. The group students should then get information about themselves (in the role of the member of the family) and also their relationship to others in the family.

4   Put 2 groups together and let them get into pairs (one student from each group). They interview each other to find out about the person and their relationship to others in the 'family'.

5   The original groups get together again and from the information they have gathered try to reconstruct and draw the family tree of the other group.

A story for the card

Level   Elementary and above

Time   30–40 min.

Preparation
Have ready one pack of playing cards per 8 students.

In class

1   Divide the class into groups of 8, sitting so they can see and hear one another.

2   Give each group one pack of cards and ask a group member to shuffle and deal them.

3   The separate groups of 8 students are to work separately and simultaneously. Student A in a given group lays down one of his/her cards. If the card is a *Spade*, then A must tell the group about something *sad* that has happened to him/her. If the Card that A lays down is a *Club*, then A tells a *lucky* experience; if the card is a *Heart*, then A tells a *romantic* experience, while a *Diamond* will evoke a story involving *money*. When player A has told his/her story, player B puts down a card and tells an appropriate personal experience, etc.

The exercise could go on for a long time, but we find it sensible to draw it to a close after about 30 min., to leave 10 min. for work on mistakes — see the main introduction.

152

The desert island leader

Level   Elementary and above

Time   25-35 min.

Preparation
Go to the bank and get enough small coins of low value to be able to give out 10 to each person in your group.

In class
1   Group the students in 8s, sitting facing each other round a table or desk top.

2   Ask them to write their names on small slips of paper and fold these over. One person in each group shuffles the slips and offers them round the group, so that each person ends up with the name of someone else in the group.

3   Give each student 10 coins.

4   Explain to the students that they have been shipwrecked with their sub-group on a remote desert island. They are very lucky to have been saved but now their task is to survive on the desert island. They are very unlikely to be able to do this unless they elect as leader the most competent person available.

Tell them that each person in each sub-group is to speak for one minute, *in their new identity*, and explain why they would make the best leader. As they listen to the speaker's leadership bid, the other members of the group are to show their approval by *giving the speaker coins*, or their disapproval *by taking away coins from the speaker*. They can give or take as many coins as they like.

The person with the largest pile of coins at the end of the exercise will have won the leadership contest for their new identity (not for their own real identity).

5   As the group of 8 listen to the leadership speeches and give and grab coins, you should walk around and listen for mistakes. Write these up on the board, quietly, without interrupting the flow of the exercise.

6 Ask the students, working now as the whole class, to look at the mistakes on the board and correct the ones they can. Only correct them yourself if nobody in the group is able to.

Acknowledgement

This is a modification (the role reversal) of an exercise we learnt from Bernard Dufeu, University of Mainz.

Crisis

Level   Elementary and above

Time   30-40 min.

In class

1   Group the students in 5s and 6s. Ask each person to think of a crisis situation they have been in or that someone they know well has been in. Ask the students to list on paper the people involved in their crisis, e.g.:

me	casualty nurse
car driver	ambulance men
casualty doctor	police inspector

2   Now ask student A in each group to assign roles in their crisis to other members of the group who they feel would fit these roles. Each student is to note down in writing the roles assigned to them. Students B, C, etc. in each group do the same. Again students note down the roles assigned to them.

3   Each person in each group has now been given several roles. At this point allow people to talk about the way they have been cast — this tends to be a great relief, especially if you have not allowed discussion in the groups during the role assigning stage.

4   Finish with a milling stage in which anyone can talk to anyone — this will assuage the intense curiosity that sometimes builds up during steps 2 and 3.

Acknowledgement

Allotting roles as a discussion provoker we learnt from Bernard Dufeu and the psychodrama tradition.

Written two-way role-play

Level   Elementary and above

Time   30–40 min.

In class

1   If possible, seat the students in a big circle. If you have fixed benches the exercise can also be done with the students in their serried rows.

2   Describe a situation in which a parent is waiting up for an early teenage child to come back home at night. The clock strikes midnight and no child appears. The parent brews coffee and gets more and more worried. 2 o'clock passes. Still no teenager. Finally, at 5 past 3 the door opens and in walks the teenager. Ask the class what they would say at this moment as the parent.

3   Ask each student to write down the parental reaction that they think is most likely on a clean sheet of paper (not in an exercise book).

4   Ask each student to pass the paper to the person *on their left,* (or behind if sitting at the end of a row). The person receiving the paper is then to write the teenager's response to the parent.

5   Everybody in the room has now written the teenager's line of dialogue. Everybody now passes their bit of paper back to the person *on their right,* the person who wrote the first parental sentence. The person who wrote the first parental sentence now writes their response to the teenager, etc.

The exercise continues with each student involved in a 2-way written role-play like this:

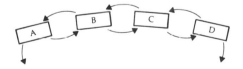

B is writing as A's parent and as C's child.
C is writing as B's parent and as D's child, etc.

6   While the writing is going on, you move round the room supplying words the students need and correcting their sentences over their shoulders. When looking at what they've written, read from the bottom of the page up, as the most recently made mistake is of the greatest interest to the student.

7   After about 20 min. of writing take in the dialogues and stick them up round the walls, so that students can read each others'.

Variations

This is an exercise frame that you can use and re-use many times over. All you have to do is find conflict situations of interest to the group, with 2 main roles. This sort of exercise is excellent in ESP situations.

Acknowledgement

We learnt this technique from Malamud & Machover (1965).

Conflicts

Level   Intermediate and above

Time   20-30 min.

In class

1   Ask the students to think of times when they have an inner conflict between what they want to do and what they must do. Get them to tell the group about these situations.

2   Ask the students to think of themselves as 2 halves, like Siamese twins but with opposing feelings and opinions.

3   Put the following pairs on the blackboard:

don't dare to   _____   must
ought to   _____   don't want to
can't   _____   want to

Tell each student to write a dialogue between the conflicting halves of him/herself.

4   Hang the dialogues on the walls so students have the opportunity to read what others have written and compare situations of conflict.

Days of the week

Level   Elementary and above

Time   15-20 min.

In class

1   Write the days of the week on the blackboard.

2   Ask the students to copy the days of the week on a piece of paper beginning with the day they like best and ending with the day they like least.

3   Pair the students and get them to compare their lists and to comment on the reason for ranking the days as they did.

4   While the students are talking to their partners, write on the blackboard, 'Would this order have been the same when you were a small child; 5 years ago; and will it change in the future?'

5   Draw the students' attention to these new points for discussion and let them continue talking for a further 5 minutes. Don't let the discussion flag.

When it happened

Level   Elementary and above

Time   30-40 min.

Preparation

Copy the 'board' opposite so that you can give out one board to every 5 or 6 students. Have dice ready so that you can give out one to every 5 or 6 students.

In class

1   Group the students in 5s or 6s. Give each group a board and a die. Tell each student to find a coin or small object to represent him/herself on the board.

2 Explain that the figures on the board represent the years of the students' lives. When Student A in each group throws the die they must tell the group something that happened in the year they have landed on. If A throws a 5, then they are to tell the group something that happened to them in the fifth year of their life.

3 At a given point in the game, students will move from the past into the future and will start saying things like: 'When I'm ... I'll...

The 'When it happened' board

100	99	98	97	96	95	94	93	92	91
81	82	83	84	85	86	87	88	89	90
80	79	78	77	76	75	74	73	72	71
61	62	63	64	65	66	67	68	69	70
60	59	58	57	56	55	54	53	52	51
41	42	43	44	45	46	47	48	49	50
40	39	38	37	36	35	34	33	32	31
21	22	23	24	25	26	27	28	29	30
20	19	18	17	16	15	14	13	12	11
1	2	3	4	5	6	7	8	9	10

Variations

The board shown on the previous page is a 'lifetime' board. If your students are 16-year-olds you may decide to make a board focussing mainly on the previous 8 years of their lives. It might look like this:

By varying the numbering on the board you can invite the students to focus on specific periods of their lives.

If you are working with middle-aged students and have given them a 'lifetime' board but want them to travel through time fairly fast, give each group 2 dice.

24	23	22	21	20	19	18
15	15	15	16	16	16	17
14	14	14	13	13	13	12
10	10	11	11	11	12	12
10	9	9	9	8	8	8
1	2	3	4	5	6	7

Shapes I belong to

Level   Elementary and above

Time   30 min.

In class

1   Invite the students to think of all the groups and communities they belong to: nuclear family, extended family, church groups, interest groups, work groups, school societies, political groups, choirs, sports teams, etc.

Now ask them to each take a sheet of paper and draw shapes to represent 4 or 5 of the groups to which they belong. Ask them also to mark their position within each group with a cross. This drawing work should be done silently and without communicating with neighbours.

2   Pair the students and ask them to explain to their partner why they have chosen a particular shape to symbolise a group they belong to. Also ask them to explain why they positioned themselves where they did within the group/shape.

3   Ask the students to pair off and explain a couple more times.

NB *In Step 1 the easiest way to make clear what you want the students to do would be to give an example of a group you belong to and a shape you would assign to it. The danger of giving a clear, personal example is that you may condition the way they do their thinking. If your shape is a firmly drawn triangle, they may feel that only precise geometrical shapes are being implicitly asked for. If you draw a bulbous balloon-like shape, they may equally well think that this is what you expect them to draw.*

We feel that you should explain the exercise but not *exemplify it; however, this is not a hard-and-fast rule.*

Acknowledgement

This idea came from the Colorado Psychodrama Warm Up Box, 1978.

Your places

Level   Elementary and above

Time   20-30 min.

In class

1   Ask the students to each pick 4 places, in either their town, their country or the world, that they know well and often go to. Ask them to sketch a map or a plan showing these places.

2   Now ask them to close their eyes and bring to mind a view connected with each place, a view seen from a habitual vantage point, e.g. a window, a place in a garden, a hilltop, the top of the stairs.

3   Group the students in 3s and ask them to compare maps. Ask each student to describe a view seen from, in, or around their 4 places and explain why they often go there.

Numbers in my life

Level   Elementary and above

Time   40 min.

In class

1   Pick some historical events that will be very familiar to your students and ask them to give you the dates for these, e.g.:

You: The end of the Second World War.
Students: Nineteen forty-five.

Put the dates given by the students on the blackboard and get students to repeat them, paying particular attention to stress. Change part of each date and get the new dates repeated:

1945 — 1845
1482 — 1582, and so on.

2   Now tell the students that numbers can be important in people's lives. Give them some examples from your own life. Dates that students have come up with in doing this exercise have included:

date of birth
number in the street
present and previous telephone numbers
padlock numbers
school/army roll numbers
car or bike registration numbers
numbers of important laws or decrees
important clock numbers

3   Ask the students to jot down on paper numbers that are, or have been, important in their lives.

4   Pair the students and ask them to explain the importance of their numbers to their partners.

5   Ask the students to pair off again with new partners and to tell their new partners the most interesting things about the old partner's numbers.

Acknowledgement

We learnt the idea of numbers as keys to important corners of people's lives from Mike Lavery of the 3M in-house Company School in West Germany.

In the news

Level   Intermediate and above

Time   40 min.

In class

1   Ask the students to think of 3 incidents that happened in their family in the past 10 years that would make interesting articles for a local newspaper.

2   Tell them to write a suitable headline for each article.

3   Pair the students and tell them to exchange the headlines. The partner chooses the one that appeals to them most and, taking on the role of a reporter, conducts an interview in order to get as much information about the incident as possible.

4   When each student has interviewed their partner, they continue in the role of a reporter and write the article.

Variation

Ask the students to come to the next class meeting with 12 or so recent newspaper stories in mind.

In the next class, ask students to outline recent news stories and have them suggest a heading for each one, which you write on the blackboard, e.g.:

economic problems
unemployment
a fatal accident
the death of a well-known person, etc.

Tell the students to each choose one of the headings that covers something that has recently happened in their family.

Group the students in 5s or 6s and have them tell the family news item.

Acknowledgement

The idea of putting personal, family happenings into a media frame is one we learnt from Moskowitz (1978).

They are cars

Level   Elementary and above

Time   20 min.

In class

1   Collect different makes and models of cars the students suggest on the blackboard. Get as many different types of car as you can, big, small, showy, modest, reliable, economical and so on.

2   Tell each student to write down the names of 5 friends or members of their family.

3   Ask the students to think of each person on their lists as a car and to write the make (and model if they want to) next to the person's name.

4   Pair the students and let them explain their choices to their partners. Tell them to say who the friend or relative is and why they think of them as that particular type of car.

End piece: how to stop people doing pair-work

In the introduction we explain how you may want to pair students, string-pairing and the like.

Are there civilised ways of stopping a group of 40 people when they are working in 20 pairs or in 13 triads or 8 groups of 5? Many teachers realise that clapping your hands or shouting over the sounds of the many conversations is rude. I've seen group leaders ring a little bell, sound a tambourine, flicker the lights on and off, increase the volume of background music, and so on.

A way we have found good is to interrupt the auditory work with a visual signal. When he or she decides to bring the group back together at the end of a pair-work phase, the teacher simply raises his/her hand, silently. The students who first spot the teacher's raised hand raise theirs. Slowly a forest of hands goes up. The pair-work is done and the group is silent.

Interrupting auditory work with a visual signal is more respectful than coming in loudly with some sort of noise. The least involved people will put their hands up first, leaving time for the more involved to surface.

We have known classes where this system of control became democratised, with the shortest-attention-span student initiating the end of the pair-work phase. Democracy can mess up the gentlest of authoritarian ideas!

Christine and *Mario*

Bibliography

Pfeiffer, J. W. and Jones, J. E. (eds), *A Handbook of Structured Experiences for Human Relations Training, Vols. I-VIII*, University Associates, La Jolla, California.

Moskowitz, G. (1978), *Caring and Sharing in the Foreign Language Classroom*, Newbury House.

Morgan and Rinvolucri (1986), *Vocabulary*, Oxford University Press.

Smith, Maury (1977), *Value Classification*, University Associates.

Wattenmaker, B. S. and Wilson, V. (1980), *A Guidebook for Teaching English as a Second Language*, Allyn and Bacon, Boston.

Leveton, Eva (1977), *Psychodrama for the Timid Clinician*, Springer Publishing Co., New York.

Stevens, J. O. (1971), *Awareness, Exploring, Experimenting, Experiencing*, Real People Press.

Sion, Chris (ed.) (1985), *Recipes for Tired Teachers*, Addison Wesley.

Spolin, Viola (1973), *Improvisation for the Theatre*, Pitman.

The Colorado Psychodrama Warm Up Box (1978).

Malamud, Daniel and Machover, S. (1965), *Towards Self-Understanding*, Charles C. Thomas, Illinois.

Wright, Andrew, Betteridge, David and Buckby, Michael (1979), *Games for Language Learning*, Cambridge University Press.

List of activities

169

Grammar index

Index of levels

Lower intermediate

Intermediate

Post-beginners

Upper intermediate